WRESTLING ACTION FIGURES OF THE EARLY 1990s

Kevin Williams

AMBERLEY

First published 2019

Amberley Publishing
The Hill, Stroud
Gloucestershire, GL5 4EP

www.amberley-books.com

Copyright © Kevin Williams, 2019

The right of Kevin Williams to be identified as the Author of this work has been asserted in accordance with the Copyrights, Designs and Patents Act 1988.

ISBN 978 1 4456 9298 2 (print)
ISBN 978 1 4456 9299 9 (ebook)

All rights reserved. No part of this book may be reprinted or reproduced or utilised in any form or by any electronic, mechanical or other means, now known or hereafter invented, including photocopying and recording, or in any information storage or retrieval system, without the permission in writing from the Publishers.

British Library Cataloguing in Publication Data.
A catalogue record for this book is available from the British Library.

Typeset in 10pt on 13pt Celeste.
Typesetting by Aura Technology and Software Services, India. Printed in the UK.

Appointed GPSR EU Representative: Easy Access System Europe Oü, 16879218
Address: Mustamäe tee 50, 10621, Tallinn, Estonia
Contact Details: gpsr.requests@easproject.com, +358 40 500 3575

Contents

Introduction	5
Series 1	6
Series 2	16
Tag Team Series 1	21
Tag Team Series 2	24
Series 3	26
Bootlegs	34
Series 4	36
Error Cards and Action Figures	40
Series 5	44
Production	50
Series 6	53
Funskool	57
Series 7	60
Series 8	66
Accessories and Other Goodies	70
Series 9	75
Series 10	79
Series 11	84
Mail Away/Bagged Action Figures	90
Series 12 and Beyond	95

Introduction

Hello and welcome to the wrestling figures of the 1990s. This book solely focuses on the greatest toy line to ever exist: the WWE Hasbro wrestling figure line. These wrestling figures were made for a short period between 1990 and 1994 and would go on to be a huge success for both parties.

In this book you will find an in-depth look at my personal collection, plus snippets of information, and take a closer look at what should have been for the entire series.

Not only are these toys memories from my childhood, they spanned the globe, attracting a huge fan base. The 1990s were a good time to be alive and bring back good memories from an eccentric era.

Star Wars, Masters of the Universe, GI Joe, Teenage Mutant Ninja Turtles, Power Rangers and Barbie, to name a few, have been given the limelight. This time it's the WWE Hasbro wrestling figures turn, the future of toy collecting.

Be prepared grapple fans and enjoy the story of the wrestling figures of the early 1990s.

Series 1

Hulk Hogan No. 1
Ultimate Warrior No. 1
Ax of Demolition
Smash of Demolition
Ravishing Rick Rude
Big Bossman No. 1 (with nightstick)
Jack 'The Snake' Roberts (with Damien)
Macho Man Randy Savage No. 1
Akeem
'Million Dollar Man' Ted Dibiase No. 1 (with million-dollar belt)
Andre the Giant
Brutus 'The Barber' Beefcake No. 1 (with Sheers)

This is where it all begins. During the late summer of 1990 the UK sees its first batch of wrestling figures. Advertisements on TV and in newspapers made for an exciting summer as the hunt had started for series 1.

Series 1 was a massive success and it instantly won over a captive audience. They soon became the talking point of every school playground. At that point wrestling in general was at an all-time high. WWE had Hulk Hogan and the Ultimate Warrior waving its flag while the competition had Sting and Ric Flair. You couldn't escape wrestling and it became a part of your life. Only years later do you realise how good you had it.

What is surprising is the popularity of the toys. They're world renowned and millions must have been sold globally. It is, perhaps, the last great toy line before the internet. It was a different approach to collecting and a connection people under the age of thirty years old will never truly understand.

Brutus 'The Barber' Beefcake
The huge glaring eyes immediately hit you as you take a closer look at Brutus 'The Barber' Beefcake. If it's not the eyes, then the purple leggings will surely get a hold of you. This is a fine example of the work from the WWE Hasbro line. The toy was super popular back in 1990 and every toyshop stocked this action figure. Today, in 2019, it's fairly easy to come by.

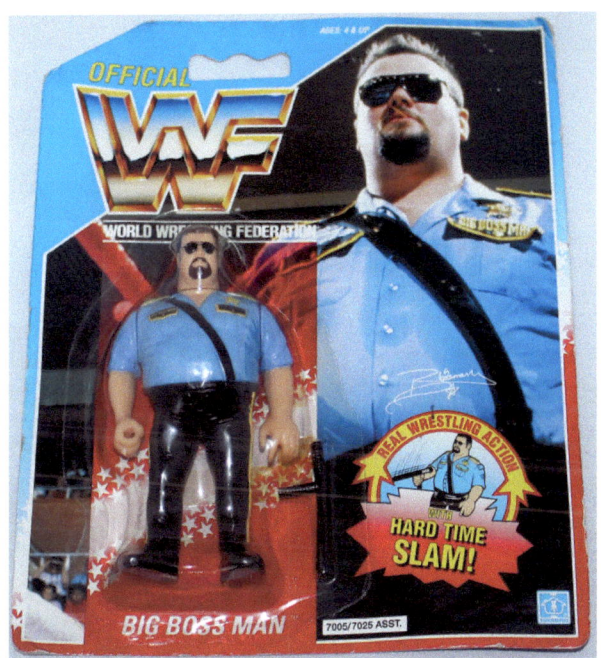

Big Bossman
During the process of production Big Bossman and Akeem split from the tag team the Twin Towers, leaving Hasbro in a sticky situation. Everything had been set for the release of Bossman as the villain, but that changed when the tag team split up. He would turn good guy while Akeem remained hated by the faithful. Hasbro had dispatched low quantities of Big Bossman and Akeem, with bio cards stating, 'A member of the tag team the Twin Towers' shortly after. That was changed and thereafter that sentence was erased. A strictly limited run had made it to completion. However, the action figure comes complete with nightstick, a quality addition. Look at the backing card and you will notice a butterfly hook, which was used for hanging the wrestling figures on shelves. Usually a 'J' hook is used. The butterfly hook was only found on UK wrestling figures for this toy line.

Akeem

Appearing in his full ring entrance attire, Akeem's action figure was never easy to find. The fact he was a mid-card competitor left his merchandise less desirable compared to other top performers. The same outcome occurs with the biography card issue as former tag team partner the Big Bossman. Versions with the sentence 'A member of the tag team the Twin Towers' survive, but only in limited amounts. Other biography cards are out there and easier to find. Everything here is within proportion and is of the quality standard, but again finding Akeem in an acceptable condition is hard. Paint wear to the attire appears regularly and the backing card often creases and bends. The trick to owning this increasingly rare toy is its condition.

Ravishing Rick Rude

This action figure is clever in a few ways. Firstly, you could perform a headlock and then fire a closed fist to the face of the opponent, or you could lift up the right arm and deliver the deadly rude awakening finishing move. No doubt versatility played its part with most action figures. The slim physique of the piece masks that of Rick Rude. The only let-down is the purple and black tights. Hasbro opted for cost-effective ring tights, because at that time Rude wore lavish ring wear that often featured multiple colours.

Ax

Ax and Smash were sold separately and not offered in the tag team twin packs. They sneak into series 1, but shortly after they would either be repackaged as different wrestlers or released from their contracts.

The action figure Ax doesn't replicate his in-ring ability in any way really; there is no memory of him ever being a heavyweight slamming wrestler. Ax was a more technical wrestler and used his grappling skills. The clothesline manoeuvre Crush uses from the tag team set was originally designed for Ax, but somewhere along the line plans were changed. Other than the mechanism issue the toy fits well. The ring attire and body garment are studded, focusing on the in-depth detail.

Smash

Similar to Ax, Smash's action figure mirrors the man in question and is an excellent creation. That right-armed wind-up punch spring-loaded action figure became popular throughout the line and in total eight wrestlers had this technique. Both demolition figures are becoming difficult to find with mint condition cards.

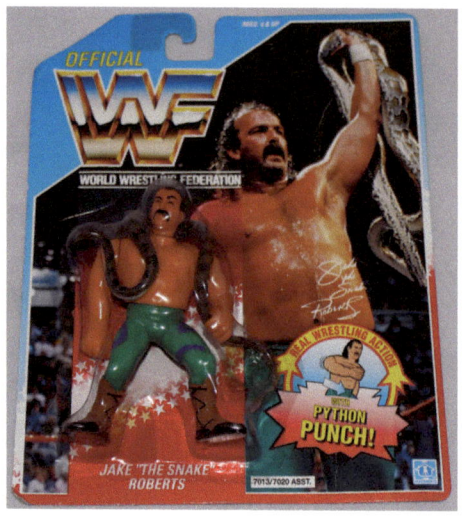

Jake 'The Snake' Roberts with Damien
Perhaps one of the most underrated wrestlers of our generation, it is a detailed action figure with, in my opinion, the coolest action figure accessory ever made. Jake's left hand is modelled in such way that he can handle his pet snake Damien. After his matches he would often let Damien loose onto his opponent, creating fear while bringing the audience to their feet. Often that after-match scene became more popular than the matches, especially concerning bouts with Andre the Giant. Recreating the scenes with the toys brought home the realness they had. Adding the snake-skinned textured boots, exceptional head sculpting and the python punch mechanism, Jake Roberts action figure grew into one of the most popular toys of the 1990s.

Hulk Hogan
Possibly the most common of all wrestling figures produced from this period, Hulk sports the famous red and yellow wrestling gear. This action figure kick-started everything for the toy line. As Hulk Hogan was the poster boy for wrestling and was known worldwide in and out of the ring, huge quantities of this toy flooded the market in every form. From mail promotions to wrestling ring exclusives, the toy would even sneak into series 3 due to its popularity. Figures have surfaced featuring all yellow and missing the red colouring on the knee pads.

Andre The Giant
One of the stand-out features of Andre's action figure is the oversizing of his body parts: the hands, head and body are larger than usual toys but that's no mistake; that's down to the detailed skill of the sculpting team at Hasbro. Andre the Giant was born with acromegaly, a cause of giantism due to a misfunctioning pituitary gland, which left him larger than life and a giant, standing at 7 feet 5 inches. Andre's wrestling figure has a headbutt motion manoeuvre, which was a great touch because in his latter days his in-ring ability slowed down and a headbutt was one of his memorable attacks. The TV commercial shows the toy with a twisting waistline, which had been removed possibly due to practicalities. An English mint-condition card version of Andre The Giant comes with a heavy price. Many action figures from series 1 were quickly opened and used in role play, and children had no desire to keeping the toys carded.

Macho Man Randy Savage
It is no surprise that former Intercontinental and Heavyweight champion Macho Man Randy Savage is included. The backing card is a beautiful piece, illustrating the Macho Man at his peak. This action figure was always fun to own. Three types of wrestling moves could be performed with this style of wrestling figure: firstly, a double axe handle effect, secondly a drop kick if you clung onto one of the action figures arms and finally and more noted a flying elbow off the top rope. A prototype version exists thanks to Matt Cardona. Instead of the orange trunks and yellow knee pads, an all-green colour is seen. It falls into the holy grail category and only one exists.

11

'Million Dollar Man' Ted Dibiase

The blonde locks with an overconfident beard, the black tuxedo only a millionaire could fashion and then the Million Dollar belt. The wind-up Million Dollar Punch could really leave a sting on the finger if you didn't execute the mechanism correctly. One simple wind-up had a minimal effect, so as a child you had to give it your all and go for two whole wind-up circles so that the mechanism nearly took off the head of the opponent. Playing with wrestling figures as a child was not as straight forward as you think – there's a technique involved. The first of three Ted Dibiase, who would you choose as your favourite?

Ultimate Warrior

Everyone must start somewhere, and this is it for me, The Ultimate Warrior was my hero and I made sure the first action figure I purchased was this one. Although a great toy, only years later did we find out that changes were made to the original design. Firstly, the green weightlifting belt moulded to the lower abdomen is bizarre. Although the Warrior was a weightlifter, he never appeared wearing any kind of weightlifting implements. Thanks to Zombie Sailor (a well-respected collector of the line) we now know the weightlifting belt mould was initially intended to be the Intercontinental championship belt fans all wanted. Hasbro drawings show this. That plan had been scrapped due to the Ultimate Warrior forfeiting the Intercontinental belt in April 1990.

Secondly, thanks to the Michael Jordan of the wrestling figure collecting world, Matt Cardona has shared images from his personal collection. The Ultimate Warrior action figure he owns is a standard tag factory sample, which has purple knee pads, not pink. That design got quickly altered early on, making the purple knee pads sample a one-off.

Finally, the last variant comes on the backing card. Photographed is the bio card that reads, 'Is the WWF Intercontinental Champion'. This is the early release backing card version, which would soon be changed to 'Won the WWF Championship title at Wrestle Mania VI'. That being said, the bio card that mentions the Ultimate Warrior as the Intercontinental champion is the hardest of the two to find.

The evidence shown and the information given, plus promoting the Ultimate Warrior as Intercontinental champion, could very possibly mean that there were plans for an Intercontinental title, to be released with the Warrior. The adjustments in biography cards is a more satisfying argument.

Wrestling Rings

Coinciding with series 1 of the WWE Hasbro action figures, the wrestling ring made for the perfect Christmas present in the winter of 1990. After all it would be a foolish move to release 101 wrestling figures and not have a wrestling ring for them to compete in. The all-blue wrestling ring measured 34 cm × 34 cm and 16 cm high, coming complete with a ringside flag and championship belt. The ropes could wear thin in time and the decals could obtain damage but overall the wrestling ring is a heavy-duty, durable and fun wrestling ring.

Variants to the traditional blue wrestling ring do exist and the main change is on the corner ring posts. Pictured above are black ring posts with a square top. Other known variants have all-blue ring posts with square tops, and again there is the round top version with no square top platform. They are known as the round top ring posts and they come in blue and black. The round top ring post wrestling rings are much harder to find compared to the square top objects. Why there are variants is unknown, but it is likely due to health and safety issues.

Blue slots are seen on the ring skirt (side of ring). Many people believe this to be in place for the possibility of a steel cage. Nothing has suggested that was the plan, even though that would have been a nice addition. Around 1992, wrestling rings became available with a sound module. It is all blue and eight buttons offered various wrestling terminologies.

King of the Ring Wrestling Ring

The year 1993 saw the introduction of the King of the Ring wrestling ring, an unusual all-yellow ring with red ring posts. The King of the Ring logo is pictured centre, and nothing changes from that of the traditional blue ring in terms of shape and size. The American flag was changed to an old WWE logo flag and the championship belt is still included.

You may ask why a yellow and red wrestling ring? Rumour has it that the ring was scheduled to be a Hulk Hogan wrestling ring. The rumour makes sense as Hulk Hogan's famous colours are yellow and red. He had left the company by 1993 so the change was easily adapted to the King of the Ring wrestling ring. Expect to pay close to £900 ($1,200) for a sealed boxed King of the Ring wrestling ring. The J. C. Penney exclusive wrestling ring comes top of the list and fetched $1,940 at auction in December 2018.

Royal Rumble Wresting Ring and Mini Figures

Late in 1991, the WWE Hasbro line introduced fans to the miniature world of wrestling figures with the Royal Rumble wrestling ring. In total eighteen miniature wrestling figures were made and six of them came exclusively with the wrestling ring. Two paddles were included with the ring, making this a two-player game. Each player would push down on the paddle, making the miniature action figures lift in the air. Whomever pushed their paddle faster and most effectively would eliminate their opponent over the top rope, just like the Royal Rumble event.

The action figures available are listed below:
Set 1 – Mr Perfect, 'Hacksaw' Jim Duggan, Rowdy Roddy Piper and Texas Tornado.
Set 2 – Brutus 'The Barber' Beefcake, The Bushwhackers and Greg 'The Hammer' Valentine.
Set 3 – The Legion of Doom and Earthquake and Typhoon from the Natural Disasters.

The six exclusive miniature wrestling figures accompanying the wrestling ring were 'Million Dollar Man' Ted Dibiase, Hulk Hogan, the Big Bossman, 'Macho King' Randy Savage, Sgt Slaughter and Jake 'The Snake' Roberts. The miniature figures were scaled down to 2 inches per action figure compared to the standard 4.5 inches seen before. Each piece was cast in a set mould and for that there was no working mechanism. The miniature action figure sets are fairly common to collectors, unlike the wrestling ring, which is much desired and attracts big money. A sealed boxed Royal Rumble ring can fetch close to £750 ($1,000).

Series 2

Ultimate Warrior No. 2
Honky Tonk Man (with guitar)
'Million Dollar Man' Ted Dibiase No. 2 (with million-dollar belt)
'Macho King' Randy Savage No. 2 (with crown and sceptre)
Rowdy Roddy Piper
Hulk Hogan
Dusty Rhodes
'Hacksaw' Jim Duggan (with 2x4)
Superfly Jimmy Snuka

Upon the success of series 1, it didn't take long before series 2 filtered through to retail stores worldwide. The first glimpse of series 2 appeared in TV advertisements in early 1991. Roddy Piper led the advert with his enthusiasm, then each wrestler promoted their action figure in a thirty-second clip. 'New WWE action figures, so close to being in the ring, it's like being in the ring' rang home with the familiar quote.

My recollection is that series 2 and the first tag team series were released at pretty much the same time. Both sets were easy to find and became the talking point with school kids and fans worldwide.

A limited number of the series 2 action figures came with the opportunity to win tickets to Summer Slam 1991 at Madison Square Garden. These became known as Summer Slam cards due to the promotion.

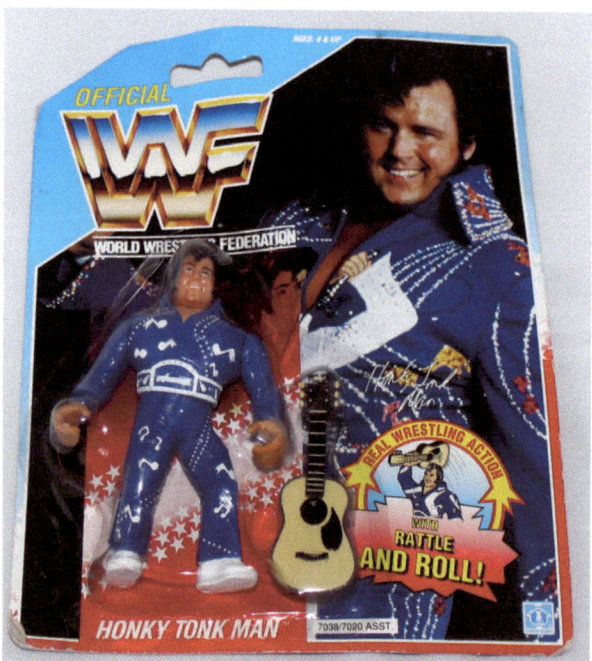

Honky Tonk Man
Originally set for purchase alongside Greg Valentine in the tag team pack the Rhythm and Blues, plans were scrapped, and the singles series 2 version replaced that. No adjustments were fashioned between the standard version and that of the tag team prototype. Smashing the guitar over wrestling figures heads emulated Honky Tonk Man's in-ring persona; after all it's the roll play that inspired a child's imagination. Without the guitar the toy was never as much fun. If there is a criticism for the action figure, then it's the lack of colour to the ring attire.

Million Dollar Man No. 2

A sombre-looking Ted Dibiase dons an all green outfit with silver tuxedo apparel and a million-dollar belt. The Million-Dollar Stomp is a wind-up motion to the right arm that triggers the movement for the right foot to stomp down onto the opponent. It was annoyingly good to play with, especially as Ted Dibiase was a bad guy at the time and that was a cheap shot to perform. You may have noticed that the belt is slightly bigger than the first belt issued with the series 1 Ted Dibiase action figure, which was due to the larger body sculpt used on this toy. It is common to find but best acquired with belt.

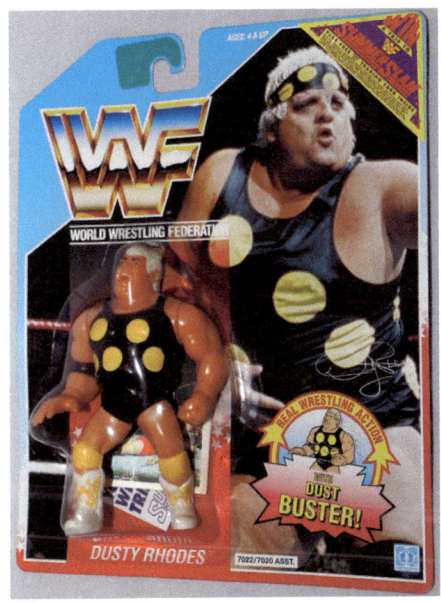

Dusty Rhodes

This was the hardest of all wrestling figures to purchase in its time. Recently, other action figures have entered the same pricing bracket, but Dusty Rhodes is deemed the defining piece by collectors. Dusty Rhodes's contract ended in early 1991, just as his wrestling figure reached retail. It was decided to halt further production, leaving a limited number in stock. Estimations of between 5,000 and 10,000 exist but the true quantity is unknown. Two carded versions exist: a Summer Slam promotion that is pictured above and a standard carded Dusty Rhodes. Both hold values of around £500 ($700) and roughly equal quantities exist of each.

Variant coloured boots that differ from white to yellow has been questioned. No clear evidence exists to class the yellow boots Dusty Rhodes as legit. However, the action figure is exceptional. It has perfectly painted ring attire and the mechanism had multiple uses. Drawing back Dusty's spring-loaded action, it performs a headbutt-like jolt. If you hold his elbow out high you execute the famous elbow to the face we all knew him for. On a sad note, UK stores never stocked the toy, which meant the high prices of eBay to find Dusty Rhodes.

Rowdy Roddy Piper
A fan favourite to many, Roddy Piper appeared everywhere at the time, from the movies to the wrestling ring. The emblematic t-shirt and rowdy kilt gave that satire cartoon glare to the figure. Very common to find and iconic to the toy line, that wind-up Piper Punch could leave a real sting to your finger if triggered incorrectly. The Piper Punch suits the Hotrod as he is remembered as a streetfighter. The world may never see another Rowdy Roddy Piper, who was a pure one-off with a huge heart. RIP.

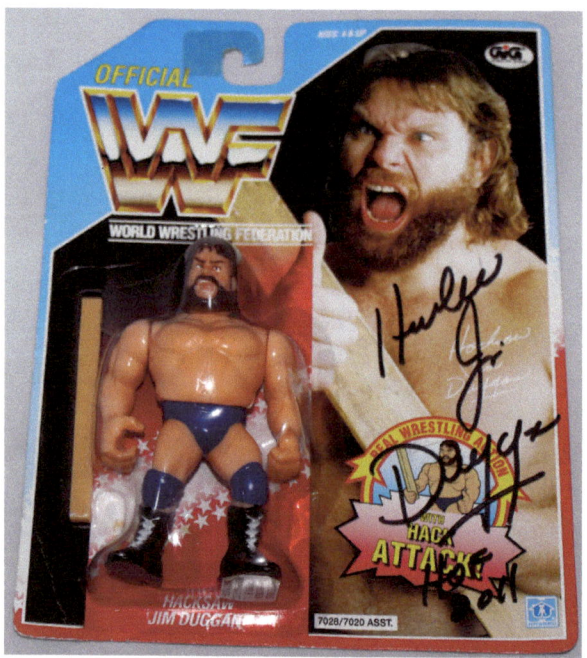

'Hacksaw' Jim Duggan
This figure is quality at its finest, possibly a hidden gem in Hacksaw Jim Duggan. This accurately made wrestling figure has it all: the crafted chest hair moulding goes unnoticed, the head sculpting is identical to the person, the working mechanism rings true and going that extra mile, Hacksaw even has cross eyes, it's that well made. What appears basic and bland truly is a masterpiece, and the 2 × 4 accessory brings back great memories too. It is full of character, a joy to play with and holds up today as a work of art.

Jimmy Snuka
Remembered for leaping from the steel cage, Jimmy Snuka's action figure had to have the jumping technique, as it wouldn't seem right to give him any other move. The leopard print outfit and skin tone are adequate, plus the big open eyes are well thought out. Check out the 'I Love U' hand gesture on the right hand.

Ultimate Warrior
This time a more accurate Ultimate Warrior helped make up series 2. No ridiculous weightlifting belt was attached, and fearsome facial expressions and a chiselled abdomen gave fans the true look of the Warrior. The prominent ring attire matched with press slam is all that's needed. It is easily obtainable and much desired by the global Ultimate Warrior fan base.

Macho King Randy Savage

The second Randy Savage action figure has a slightly toned down, more serious complexion and it's not as eye-catching compared to the series 1 version. Purple trunks, white boots and golden colour knee pads copy the Macho Man's in-ring apparel, and the item includes a removable crown and sceptre accessory. One annoying point to the Randy Savage here is the gold colouring to the glasses and the knee pads as they rubbed away easily. Acquiring this figure in pristine condition can be a task, and not many collectors are interested in the toy in poor condition.

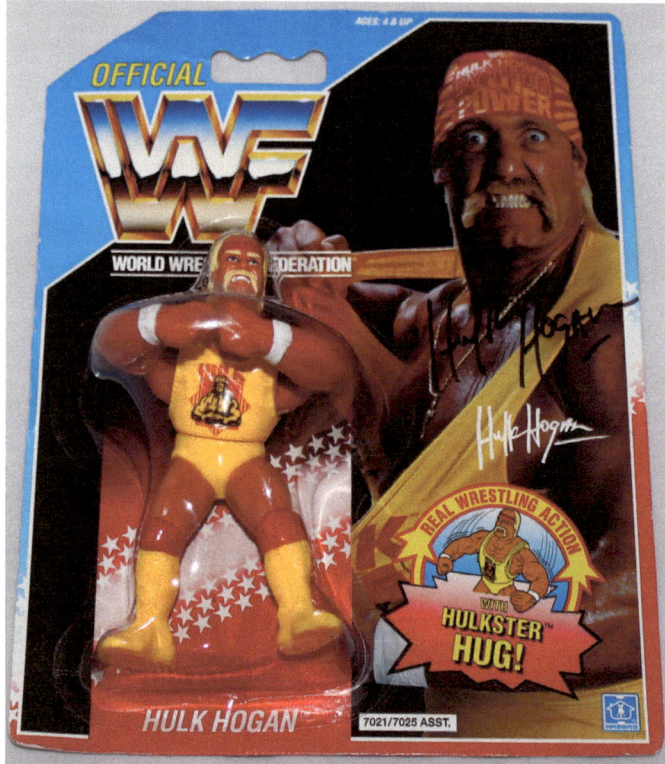

Hulk Hogan

A one-off mould for Hulk Hogan that boasts a Hulkster Hug mechanism. In reality it's showcasing the muscular physique of Hogan and is as close as fans got to seeing a shirt-ripping action figure. It's the second of eight merchandise items of Hulk Hogan from the toy line. Widely available, it frequently surfaces even today at flea markets and charity stalls due to its large scale of production. This action figure became available through various promotional offers from Silver Vision and several cereal brands. Check out the mail away chapter for more information.

Tag Team Series 1

The Rockers (Marty Jannetty and Shawn Michaels)
The Bushwhackers (Luke and Butch)
Demolition (Smash and Crush with helmets)

With the tag division at its heights, it was only right to include tag team sets. Two-pack sets were released in early 1991 and feature only five tag teams. The toys were the same size and, using the same ethos as the single release wrestlers, match in everything that stood before and after.

No tag team championship belts were made and some of the legendary tag teams were missing. The Hart Foundation, Beverley Brothers and the Natural Disasters, to name a few, could have brightened up the tag team sets.

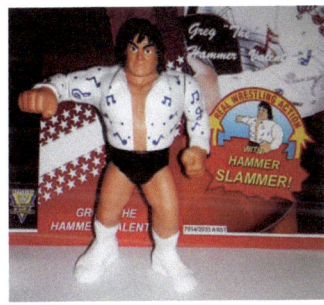

Rhythm and Blues
The one tag team that dominates the talk is the Rhythm and Blues, Greg 'The Hammer' Valentine and the Honky Tonk Man. Appearing in advertisements, the tag team was expected for release in early 1991. By the time of release, Rhythm and Blues had split up, which meant cancelling the tag team. It is understood that the tag team was very close to release but that was stopped literally weeks before the first batch of production.

Honky Tonk Mans action figure would filter into series 2, and there's no immediately noticeable changes to the toy. Greg 'The Hammer' Valentine's action figure would be a different situation. Appearing as a singles wrestler at that time, he swaps the jet-black hair for the traditional blonde and the waistcoat used in the tag team had long gone. In recent years, prototype action figures of Greg 'The Hammer' Valentine have surfaced that are modelled in his Rhythm and Blues ring attire. It's highly regarded and can sell for anything between $8,000 and $15,000.

The picture used is a custom-made effort kindly donated by Robert Coughlin. Robert would become one of the great custom-making action figure experts, and his work is respected worldwide.

The Rockers

They were a super quick high-flying tag team, who worked together fabulously, wrestling in tandem and performing in synchronisation, making wrestling appear in art form. It was no surprise Shawn Michaels would reach the level he did. He must be one of the greatest performers of our time. Marty Jannetty could have achieved somewhere close to his counterpart if it wasn't for injuries and other issues holding him back. The action figures give an excellent cartoon image of The Rockers, both with boyish good looks and childish likeness. Marty's action figure is unique, with an arm spring technique whereby both feet lift high to create a drop-kick effect. No other action figure would copy this design. Shawn Michaels has a jump action, which became familiar throughout the line. The action reminds you of the finishing move The Rockers would perform from the top rope: a diving flying fist. They were a great tag team who deserve to be included.

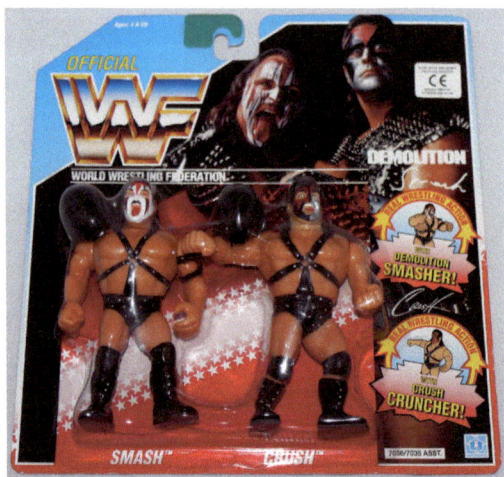

Demolition

This tag team set sees Smash and Crush included in the tag team set. Ax had to take a less active role with the tag team due to injuries, which made way for Crush to make Demolition into a three-way tag team. Two masks were added to the tag team set, something that didn't happen the first time around in series 1. It's annoying to see Smash included in this way as the figure had already been seen in series 1 – a change of face paint could have given fans just that little something different. The action figure of Crush is decent and is a nice addition. The clothesline mechanism labelled the Crush Crusher fits perfectly. The masks accessories have entered the hard-to-find category, but also watch out for custom-made examples.

Bushwhackers

Luke and Butch, The Bushwhackers, were a whacky and fun tag team to be around. Luke (left) has the Bushwhacker walk motion, which is unusual and only came with the Bushwhacker toys. Butch has a more traditional stomp action. Images of the original sketch were drawn up by ex-Hasbro artist Bart Sears. The scale of the drawing is 22 inches by 17 inches and is on large white sheet of paper. The drawing gives all sorts of information from facial expressions to mechanisms used. The sculpting team would then take from this and make up the action figures to either a standard size prototype or a larger two-up scale (two-up is twice the size of a standard action figure).

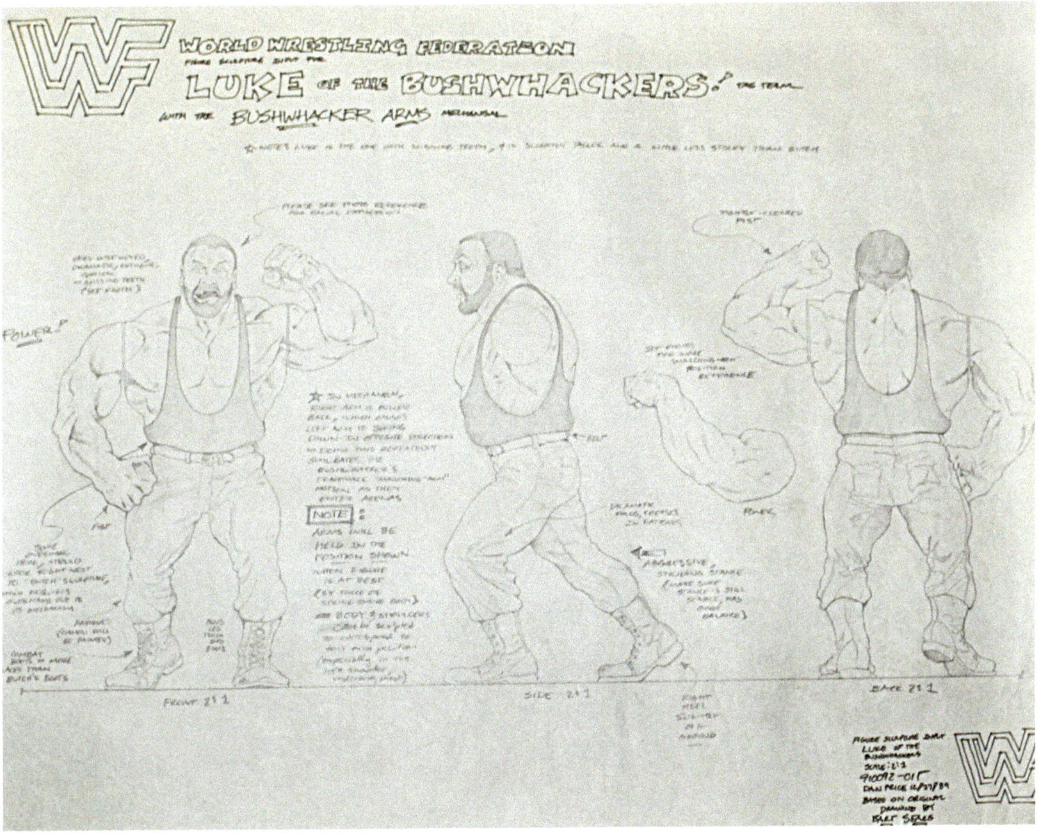

Tag Team Series 2

Legion of Doom (Hawk and Animal)
The Nasty Boys (Knobbs and Sags)

Legion of Doom
One of the most iconic wrestling tag teams ever, the Legion of Doom were famous for the mohawk hair, painted faces, the feared spikes and colossus in-ring destruction. These two were great additions to the line as they are up there in the popularity ratings, and even today they're remembered some fifteen years since retirement. Legion of Doom's spikes had to be cut short and avoided the spiky endings for health and safety reasons. Although a logical reason, I don't know anyone who wouldn't have wanted to see removable spikes.

The Nasty Boys
From head to toe, both wrestling figures portray a great likeness to the Nasty Boys. The spray-painted shirts replicate what they wore and then the well-carved wrestling boots stand out. Even though the Nasty Boys were hated in the wrestling ring, you have to appreciate this.

Series 3

Hulk Hogan
Big Bossman (with nightstick)
Greg 'The Hammer' Valentine
Koko B Ware (with Frankie)
Sgt Slaughter
Brutus 'The Barber' Beefcake (with black and silver sheers)
Texas Tornado
Typhoon
Earthquake
Ultimate Warrior
Macho Man Randy Savage
Mr Perfect

Series 3 gives us a huge batch of action figures, featuring twelve of our wrestling heroes. The series has everything here, from legends and accessories to their counterparts, and matching, as wrestling rode the crest of a wave in 1991. Stock amounts from series 3 vary, with certain areas receiving decent batches of wrestling figures while some didn't quite get the full quota. UK wrestling fans mention the availability of the Ultimate Warrior, Brutus 'The Barber' Beefcake and Koko B Ware, to name just a few, which appear to be less popular on UK shores. Reasons for this are unknown. One possibility is that shops still flooded with series 1 and 2 action figures were not so keen on taking a chance on the later action figures.

Valuations of certain wrestling figures have risen drastically over the past decade. All on English card, Ultimate Warrior is the most sought after, but Mr Perfect, Koko B Ware, Brutus 'The Barber' Beefcake and Macho Man Randy Savage have increased too. This suggests that there must have been a lower number of English language backing cards.

Ultimate Warrior
The third and final action figure of the Ultimate Warrior makes series 3. Ultimate Warrior disappeared from our TV screens in the summer of 1991, leaving fans bewildered to his whereabouts. His action figure was hitting retail just at the time of his departure. However, it has to be one of the best action figures made. The chiselled body muscle, expressive face image and sheer arm muscles outline his true likeness. Then adding the Warrior Wham movements to the mould, this, to me, is the epitome of the famous toy line.

The action figure is fairly common to find loose but owning an English language backing card version is extremely hard. Dusty Rhodes is possibly the rarest of all mint-condition card action figures, but you could place the English language version as a close second. Expect to pay close to £500 ($700) or more. There are two images for you to look at here. The action figure above is regarded as an 'Italian card' action figure whereas the version below is an 'English/US card' language. Due to the WWE's global wrestling appeal, these toys hit all four corners of the globe. Other languages are known as French and Spanish language backing cards. Plus, a dual language Canadian backing card was available, which featured French and English writing. Stickers placed on to the backing card have shown us Korean, Greek and Indian examples were available, which illustrates the scale and appeal of these wrestling figures.

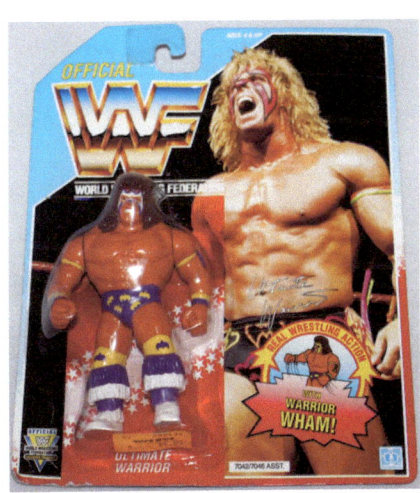

Earthquake and Typhoon

I'll put these two together, although they weren't released as a tag team The Natural Disasters, each action figure copies each other, making this an odd connection. Earthquake and Typhoon became the Natural Disasters tag team in mid-1991. Typhoon's action figure wears the tag team ring attire, but oddly Earthquake does not. I suppose we can excuse WWE Hasbro for this as the time scale between manufacturing and the tag team's formation. Bizarrely on Typhoon's biography write up he's stated as being a member of the Natural Disasters but then Earthquake is purely still a singles competitor. There is a mix up here. As both action movements were the same, all that was required was Earthquake to be decorated in his Natural Disasters wrestling gear. That being said it would have been nice to see the two action figures set apart instead of both looking alike and doing the same motion.

Mr Perfect

The first of two Mr Perfect action figures, he is wearing the popular yellow ring attire, with his curly blonde locks, and sports his finishing move the Perfect Plex. Shortly after the action figures distribution, Perfect had to take a hiatus from wrestling. During this period he would cover commentary and in 1992 he worked a fabulous angle with Ric Flair being his executive consultant.

Owning this Mr Perfect toy was such a joy. Gearing up the opposition was made simple with this action figure: simply slot the head under the right arm then wind up that left arm to slam home the Perfect Plex. If you own an English carded series 3 Mr Perfect action figure, you are no longer a small-time player. It takes some guts to pay out close to £200 ($350) for the pleasure.

The saddest part of being an old-school wrestling fan is that a lot of 1980s/90s wrestlers are no longer with us, either due to tragedy, prescription drugs or other issues. Mr Perfect passed away aged forty-four, and he and all the wrestling legends alongside him will be remembered forever.

Macho Man Randy Savage
There's no real difference between the series 3 Macho Man and the series 2 Macho King action figure. On the back of the trunks of the series 3 figure reads 'Macho Man', while series 2 reads 'Macho King'. No crown or sceptre accessories were included here. The backing card to the wrestling figures is also different.

Greg 'The Hammer' Valentine
Finally, after all the fuss, we see a Greg 'The Hammer' Valentine figure, albeit among a series 3 range. As mentioned in the tag team section, we never did see a Rhythm and Blues tag team version, only seeing this basic singles wrestler version. Enrobed in black trunks with yellow boots and the distinguished leg brace, the Hammer happened to be a shelf warmer in its day as huge volumes were produced. Take a look at the seriousness on Greg 'The Hammer' Valentine's face. Only within recent years has the price slowly begun to rise.

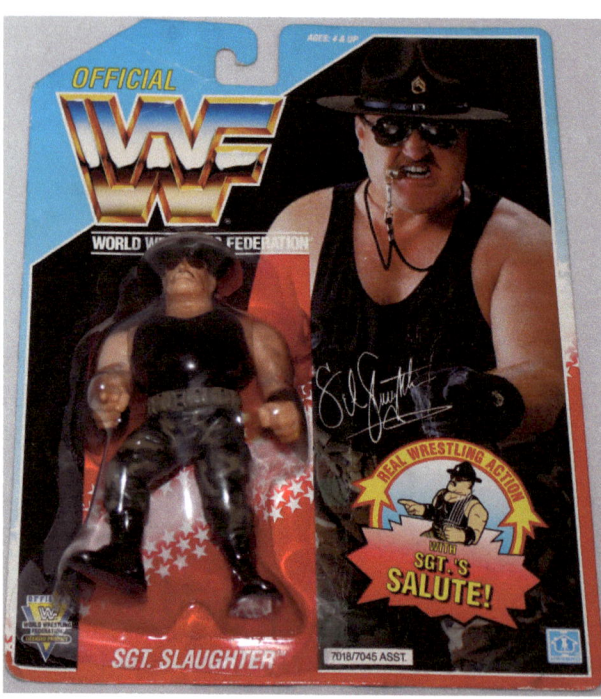

Sgt Slaughter
This is the correct mint-condition card version of Sgt Slaughter, and you can see his name printed just below the action figure. His biography card is interesting as he's described as an all-American turncoat. In 1991, he worked matches as a bad guy versus Hulk Hogan, waving the Iraqi flag right in the mist of the Gulf War. WWE had to place extra security around Sgt Slaughter as he received many death threats. Who says wrestling is fake? I don't think so. The best parts of the toy are the military uniform and the Sgt Salute wrestling action. Lifting both arms triggered Sarge into combat. The hat and sunglasses are a decent effort, and Sgt Slaughter's toy even has the big chin.

Big Bossman
Much slimmer compared to the first Big Bossman action figure, this focuses on his time as a good guy. There is no difference between the nightsticks issued with series 1 and series 3. Credibility in hand, not only did the feature look the part but also an action figure of this calibre had multiple function. We had the clothesline move, then the nightstick accessory could be used as a foreign object, and, on top of that, the Jailhouse Slam mechanism could be converted into a sidewalk slam, the Big Bossman's finishing move. These toys were never intended to be ornaments and were great to wrestle with. You had to have the brain power to take the initiative with these action figures. It bought so much creativity out in so many children.

Texas Tornado
A member of the Von Erich family, Texas Tornedo is legendary in the Dallas, Texas, area. Kerry Von Erich, the Texas Tornado, joined the WWE in 1990, and then defeated Mr Perfect at Summer Slam 1990 to win the Intercontinental Championship. The action figure has a great likeness to the Texas Tornado. The whirlwind mechanism the toy boasts recreates the finish move of the Texas Twister. What Hasbro could have done differently here is have the left hand open to a claw shape to mimic a favoured in-ring move of his. Then the toy could have twisted 360 degrees, smashing his opponent to the ground.

Koko B Ware
High-flying athlete Koko B. Ware, equipped with pet macaw Frankie, is a part of series 3. Koko was renowned for bouncing from rope to rope, turnbuckle to turnbuckle, in his lively wrestling matches. The toy is well worked out and copies that. Adjoining Koko B Ware is Frankie. The colour macaw accessory is created perfectly, the engraved feather marks adding more than just colour. Bizarrely Frankie is worth more than Koko B Ware. Unfortunately, Frankie perished in a house fire in 2002. Is Frankie the best accessory from the toy line?

Brutus 'The Barber' Beefcake
The second action figure of Brutus 'The Barber' Beefcake. With black and white zebra print tights, silver and black sheers and a glowing facial expression, the toy fits more to his time in 1990 just before his parasailing accident. Loose examples of the action figure are common, but a perfect English mint on card version is harder to come by. Due to the action figures also being released with foreign language backing card, the production numbers of the toy were fairly high, but only a smaller number survive with the English language backing card. It suffers the same fate in value as the Ultimate Warrior action figure from this series.

Hulk Hogan

Yet more Hulk Hogan merchandise. What stands out is the backing card, which has a serious look. Draped with the star-spangled banner, it is a patriotic work, possibly triggering more sales in the process. No complaints can be made about this action figure either, as the attire, physical appearance, skin tones and backing card show Hulk Hogan at his best. The suplex manoeuvre adds to the toy, giving it that larger complex. Check out the signature. Personally signed at a UK event, there is no difference between the hand-signed signature and the printed signature.

Bootlegs

Every great brand has bootlegs. WWE Hasbro is no different and has an array of 'alternative' action figures that boast many similarities to the masters. Not all of the knock-off copies of wrestling figures are illegal as some had obtained permission, licensing and action figure moulding sets from the required companies.

Various companies attempted to recreate that of WWE Hasbro, but it was Simba and Mannix who had the most visible and available alternative action figures on the market. Simba used the entire mould from Hasbro and flooded European countries, especially Germany. Mannix International Wrestling Champions, however, only used the head sculpts from the Hasbro mould, and the body sculpts are of a different kind, being bigger and much uglier. A Diesel head mould was used with Mannix and in reality, it's the closest to series 12. Custom-made wrestling figures often borrow head parts from these two companies to hone their skills.

Separate versions of a Macho Man Randy Savage and Ultimate Warrior from series 1 have surfaced and have links to Spain. Mash-ups of Demolition featuring Ax's head on a Smash body exists, but to where and to which brand is unknown to myself. Several unknown brands have appeared over time, but tracking a maker is the hard part. Below are some examples.

Believed to have links to Mexican Wrestling, but again unusual.

Mannix International Wrestling Champions body parts are totally different, but do you recognise the head sculpt? It's Lex Luger. Whether that head sculpt was set for a new series 12 Lex Luger is debatable.

A Simba action figure. You can see straight away the head sculpt is from Jake Roberts, but other body parts from the line are mixed up to make the action figure.

Series 4

British Bulldog
Bret 'The Hitman' Hart
The Undertaker
Ricky 'The Dragon' Steamboat (with wings)

Only the four action figures made up series 4. It is such a low number and has started rumours that series 4 was a stop gap. Adjoining this series, the second batch of tag team wrestling figures featuring the Legion of Doom and the Nasty Boys had become available. Plentiful amounts of action figures from series 4 flooded retail stores and each became household favourites. The great surprise of 1990s toys was that adverts reached us after the toys had hit retail, just like in this case.

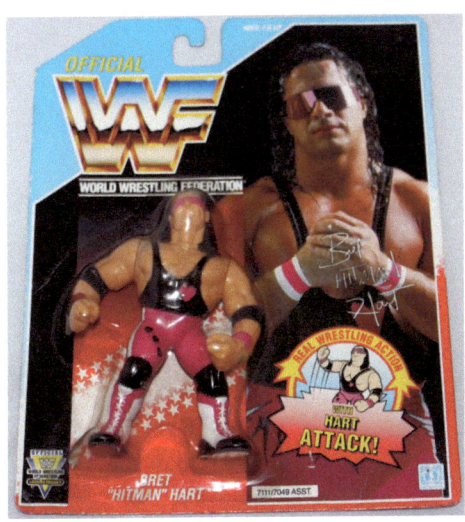

Bret 'The Hitman' Hart

Bret Hart built-up popularity after his action figure became available to the public. With the toy line at its heights and giving that ultimate conceited pose to the action figure, it soon became a must have for the collection and is a favourite among the wrestling community. Pictured here are two variant versions of the action figure. The colour of the heart on the vest of Bret can be found in two colours, pink and purple. It is said to be a more popular pink heart (above) and the slightly harder to find purple heart (below). It is unknown why there are two versions.

Word has arisen that Bret Hart frequented the Hasbro studio, aiding and supporting his wrestling figure. He exchanged cartoon drawings and must have been a fan of the line. Videos featuring Bret show he has a two-up action figure prototype version within his vault. A two-up action figure is similar to a prototype design made by Hasbro but is twice the size of normal action figures. Only one for each action figure got made. Having met Bret on three occasions, he is one of only a few wrestlers who go that extra mile to make fans happy. When signing the series 4 purple heart version MOC action figure, he commented on the remarkable condition and how older wrestling merchandise had more of an appeal to him than the newer goods available today.

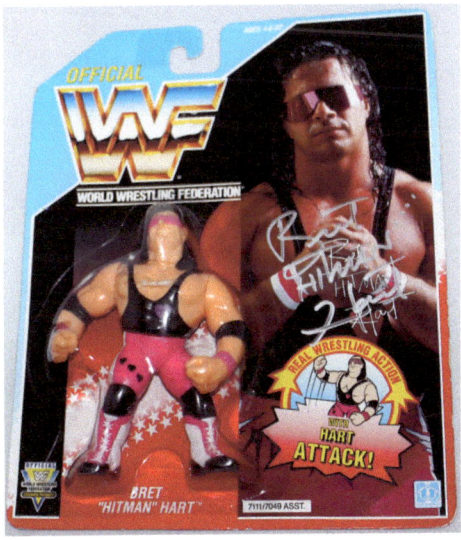

The Undertaker

The very first action figure of The Undertaker. After debuting in 1990, the career of Mark Calaway has turned him into legendary status. Playing with this action figure had so many options: you could choke out an opponent, execute choke slams and, if you're creative enough, finish the match with a tombstone.

Undertaker wears his most notorious ring attire: black ripped shirt and black tights, which had those Grim Reaper grey socks and gloves. He looked zombie-like, and it bought out the character of the dead man. Did you know the left hand of The Undertaker is carved in such a way to accommodate the distinguished urn Paul Bearer clutched during wrestling matches? Plans were scrapped and no urn became available. Neither did we see a manager's series. Paul Bearer carried the urn and was one of the great wrestling managers. The World Wrestling Federation and Hasbro missed a trick by not releasing a manager's series.

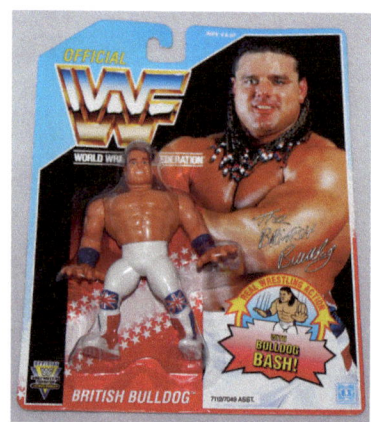

The British Bulldog

This guy needs no introduction to the British wrestling scene. He is one of the iconic guys who waved the union jack high as he stormed the globe, competing on every wrestling continent. With the braided hair and matching ring attire, it begs the question: is this the greatest action figure from the toy line? As a fellow Brit I am somewhat bias, but it is, in my opinion, the best Davey Boy Smith action figure ever made. The Bulldog Bash slamming mechanism, a recognised manoeuvre of his, is quality. Every school playground boasted the toy and it felt as if an overflow became the norm on British soul. In 2019, a mint on card Davey Boy Smith toy holds decent value. When originally sold in 1992, it never crossed my mind that this toy could fetch close to £100 some twenty-five years later.

In recent years, Ron Rudat, the famous Hasbro artist, has indicated an accessory of Winston, Davey Boy's pet bull terrier, was planned, but nothing came of it from the early design stages.

Ricky 'The Dragon' Steamboat

This jumping action figure shows The Dragon in his full wrestling attire and it never gets as much credit as it deserved. Take a closer look at the sculpted modelling work and appreciate this action figure. The modelling is accurate to the minute detail, and the scales of his outfit outlining his chest and tights are incredible, adding the same to the Dragon headwear and wrist bands. The head sculpt is astonishingly perfect too. It is an underrated example of excellence. Fans never positively accept the workmanship that went into it. The original prototype mould would have been hand-worked, with no 3D imagery or machinery. Resins, plastics, moulding clay and crafting tools were all that was needed. From then on, in the later stages, the artists painted to perfection one of the greatest wrestling figures ever made and it is not even recognised.

Error Cards and Action Figures

Error cards simply exist through the mistake from the production line at the factories. Every business in the world makes errors, no matter how big or small. An error can range from a small printing error to a total mess-up when, for instance, the wrong action figure becomes attached to the wrong backing card or body parts are totally switched around.

An error card will usually demand more money from a collector, because there is normally a low number produced or, on rare occasion, only one of one of the errors are known to exist.

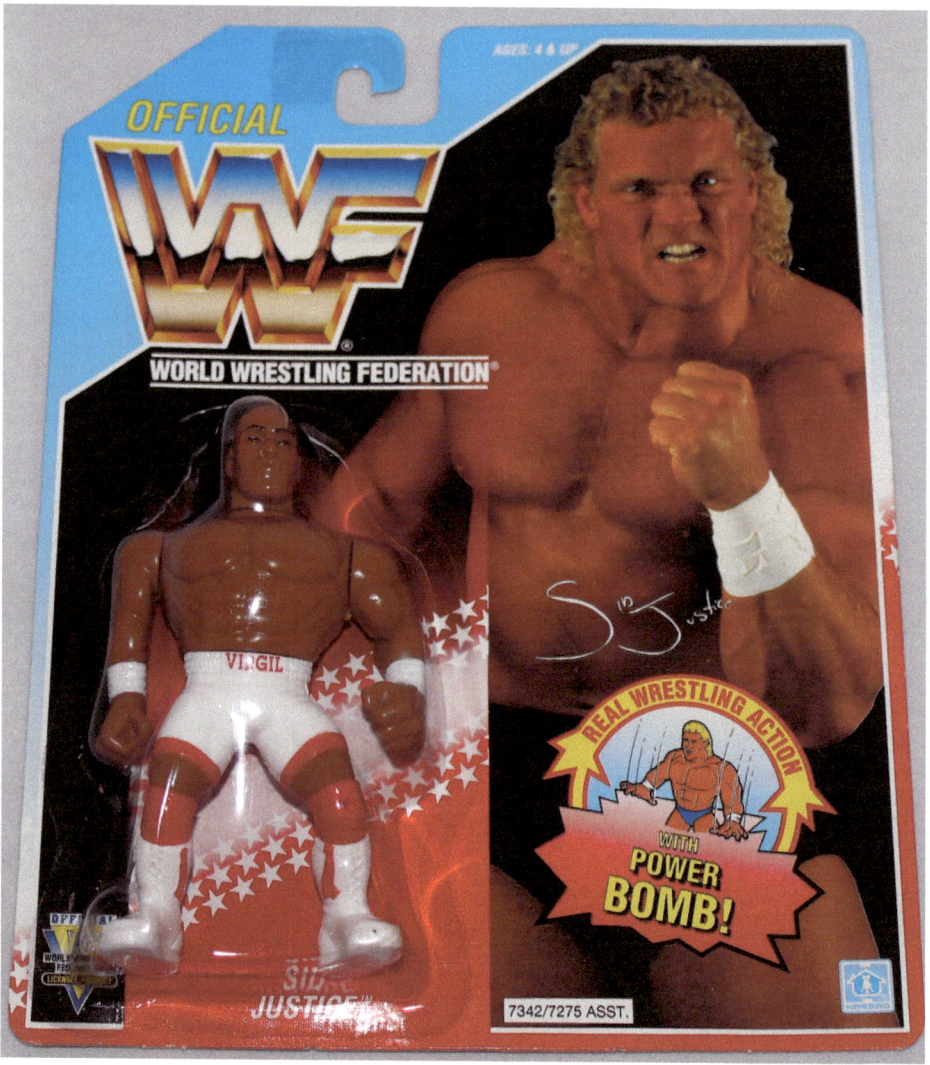

Pictured here is a Virgil action figure attached to a Sid Justice backing card. It doesn't take a genius to spot this simple mistake.

Here again, The Undertaker action figure sits firmly attached to the Bret 'The Hitman' Hart action figure. An error card of this nature will attract a larger interest. Yes, like the Virgil/Sid Justice error card it's a one off, but the pro-wrestlers in question have a huge fan base and both are legendary in the world of wrestling.

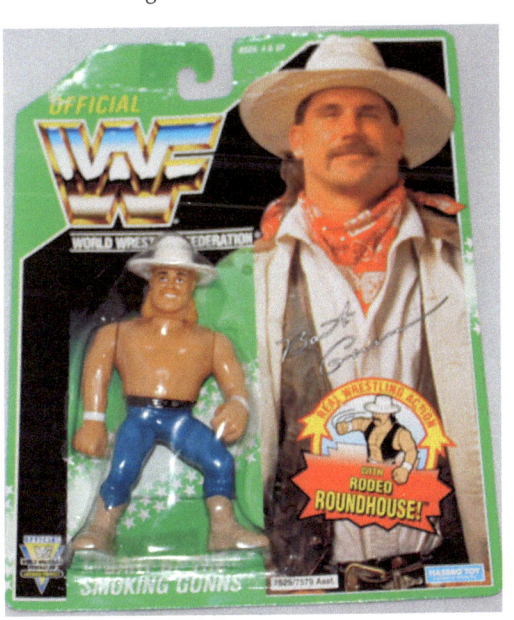

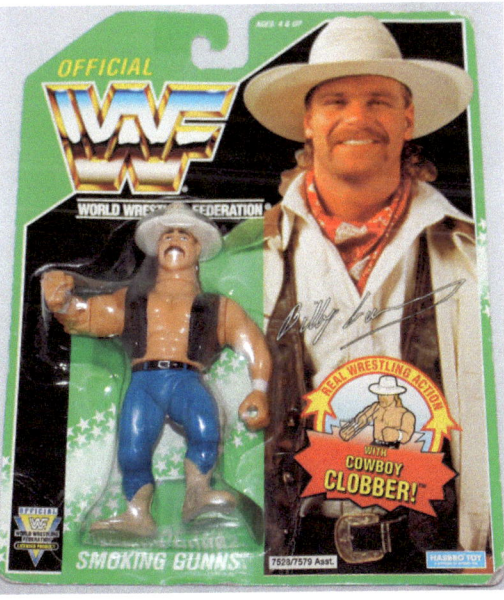

The Smoking Gunn's error cards tag team. Can you notice the error/mistake here? Billy Gunn is attached to a Bart Gunn backing card and vice versa. It's an easy factory mistake to make as both guys look similar and the action figures aren't too far apart.

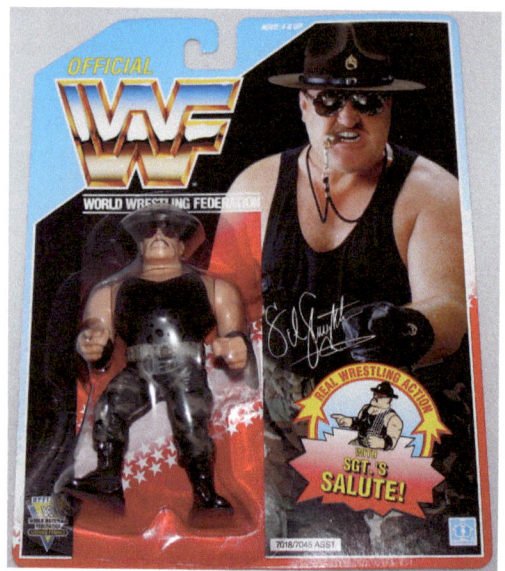 

This one is a hard-to-notice error example, if you are not a serious collector of the line. Where the action figure sits, there should be Sgt Slaughter's name. Rumour has it that 250 slipped through quality control and a handful still exist today. The correct product is situated on the right.

Error cards can include bonus accessories. Instead of one nightstick you may have two.

Notice the name of Crush is under the Smash action figure and Smash is written under the action figure of Crush, a common error found on many foreign language backing cards.

Finally, you can see here the action figure is misaligned to the centre. Situated more right of central, an unusual error and various misaligned action figures pop up from time to time. More error cards have surfaced and the great collectors throughout the world have some whacky examples.
Be careful of sun damaged action figures. Occasionally traders will pass them off as error action figures, but in fact the action figure has sat close to sunlight, which has changed its colour.

Series 5

Macho Man Randy Savage
Sid Justice
IRS (Irwin R. Schyster)
Skinner
The Mountie (with cattle prod)
The Warlord
Rick 'The Model' Martel
Virgil
Jim 'The Anvil' Neidhart
Hulk Hogan No. 4

Ten action figures feature in series 5 and some legendary wrestlers make up the set. Series 5 would hit UK retail right at its peak – 1992. Summer Slam 1992 used Wembley Stadium as its venue and the entire country was engulfed with wrestling. 80,355 people filled Wembley that day to see British Bulldog beat his brother-in-law Bret 'The Hitman' Hart for the Intercontinental title.

As Summer Slam 1992 happened, series 5 would be successful and become familiar with most wrestling fans. Advertisements for the action figures were seen everywhere, from TV commercials to magazines. It was no wonder they became toy of the year in 1992.

The attraction was the wide variety of colours and fresh mouldings used for the legends of wrestling. Looking through the list of wrestlers who made series 5, you will see that the wrestlers involved later become icons of the sport. Whether they became champions, future hall of famers or were remembered for their work, this is where the line hit the top.

The Mountie

The proud Canadian Jacques Rougeau Jr is decorated in the full Royal Canadian Mounted Police attire, aiming to enforce the law. This well-crafted action figure comes complete with the shock stick cattle prod accessory. The original shows a red and yellow colour and not black.
The beauty of your childhood was holding wrestling matches against co-wrestlers to declare who was your champion. The Mountie had an on-screen TV battle with the Big Bossman, and this carried over to the action figures.

Jim 'The Anvil' Neidhart

A singles wrestling version of Jim 'The Anvil' Neidhart appears in series 5. I don't know any wrestling fan who wouldn't have wanted to see him in a tag team set with Bret 'The Hitman' Hart. Matching the ring costume he wore when in the tag team the New Foundation, Neidhart has a happy smiling face just like how fans remember him. The famous beard stroke is not quite possible as these action figures weren't quite as flexible. The larger physique is an accurate representation of Jim and his no messing, rough and ready, play around with the big anvil and you're getting hurt look.

    Forever remembered as one half of the greatest tag teams ever: the Hart Foundation. Maybe one day WWE and Mattel could give us a Hart Foundation tag team set.

IRS

Irwin R. Schyster suited up as a tax collector, creating the hate for a villain. This ghostly looking action figure was never going to be a top seller as every fan hated IRS. Even though Hasbro did an excellent job with the toy, due to the fact he was a bad guy wrestling fans would certainly think twice about purchasing the merchandise. Most toy stores were left with an abundance of IRS action figures and it's safe to say it was a shelf warmer. Seeing as no referee had been included in the line, Irwin R. Schyster would fit in perfectly, so after all there was a use. Today, a mint on card action figure is steadily increasing in value.

Virgil

Take a closer look at the excellent work the sculpting team have done on this action figure. It certainly fits the bill as the best Virgil/Mike Jones action figure, but does it come close to the best from the toy line? That's up to you to decide, but it never gets enough credit. The boxing ring attire matches that of mid-1991. Long striped trousers may have been a better choice as he is remembered more for wearing them. The figure is easily found today.

'Macho Man' Randy Savage

The final version of 'Macho Man' Randy Savage. Many collectors like to call this the Cowboy Macho Man wrestling figure. The multi-coloured wrestling attire is a focal point, nicely fitting in with the backing card as both wrestling attires match. 'Oh Yeah' quotes are on display, pointing out one of his famous catchphrases. A jumping action figure of the Macho Man made for a quality variant to the other three figures already seen. You can't help but pay attention to the ring attire on this figure: the tassels below each arm, vibrant green cowboy hat and multi-colour bursts on the ring costume. This Macho Man action figure is deemed most valuable from the entirety of series 5.

Sid Justice

In 1992, Sid Justice battled Hulk Hogan at WrestleMania VIII, which should have been the match that catapulted his career even further, as he had everything to be a top wrestling star. Things never worked out and there's nothing much to mention until his return in 1996. The blue and black ring attire is reminiscent of 1992 – Hasbro got that right – and the curly blonde locks are there to be seen too. What's truly awesome about the Sid Justice action figure is the Power Bomb wrestling move it performs. Every wrestler feared the Power Bomb.

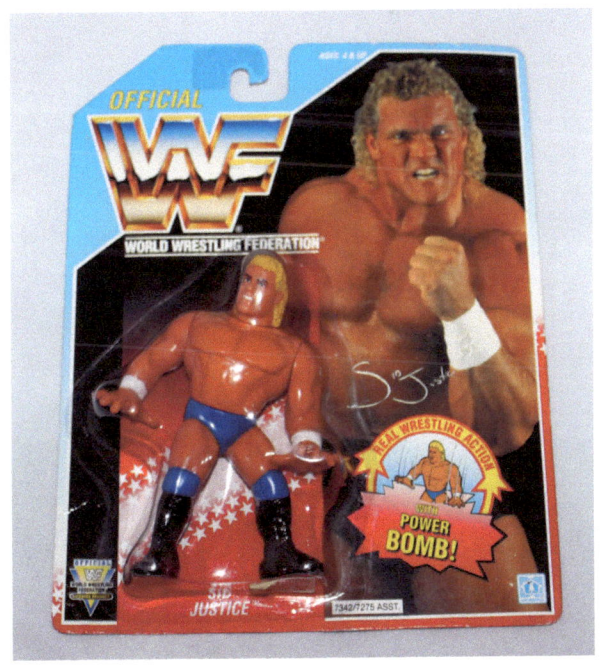

Warlord
Albeit a great toy, the Warlord action figure was annoying in some respects but beautiful in others. The upper armour and face mask were firmly attached and not removable. Warlord had the biggest physique in the company and they never capitalised on that as the armour hides a good portion of it. To be fair, if the armour and mask were demountable, it's likely they would have been lost. Another sad point is he's missing the 'W' spear he carried to matches, but let's not take away everything else from the figure. As a collector and even though I'm not an owner, it has been a pleasure seeing the recent material that has arisen about the Warlord action figure. Drawings, prototypes, test shots and a two-up action figure are there in view.

Hulk Hogan
The fourth instalment of Hulk Hogan, this time the Hulkster appears shirtless and sports the long-established bandana, adding the Hulkster Slam! One could add the skin tone has a slightly pale complexion considering he appears well tanned. There is nothing to add in depth here other than it's a great action figure from series 5.

'The Model' Rick Martel

This charmingly modelled head sculpt of Rick Martel stands out. With the slicked back hair and flamboyant smile, this action figure oozes arrogance. A seductive pose from the action figure and wearing a glittering pink attire, it makes it a little bit more treasured. Packaging plays an important role here. The Real Wrestling Action image reads 'with Arrogance Splash!'. It refers to the cologne Rick Martel wafted towards his opponent during matches as a distraction. We needed his bottle of arrogance as an accessory to add to the fun.

Skinner

Another fantastic action figure here in Skinner. Perfectly balanced and well structured, there's no denying the action figure looks identical to the man in person. There's everything to love here, from the hat to the patterned engraved shirt. The prototype images advertise Skinner wearing a maroon brown shirt, but by the time product had started the shirt changed to a solid green colour. Everything else remained the same.

The mechanism, the same style as Ultimate Warrior series 3 – push the head down, feet go in and then arms wave about like a maniac. It had to be a maniac as Skinner wrestled crocodiles for a living.

Production

This chapter scratches the surface on the production side of business. Adding to this, items in this section have been known to attract serious money. It's a book in itself!

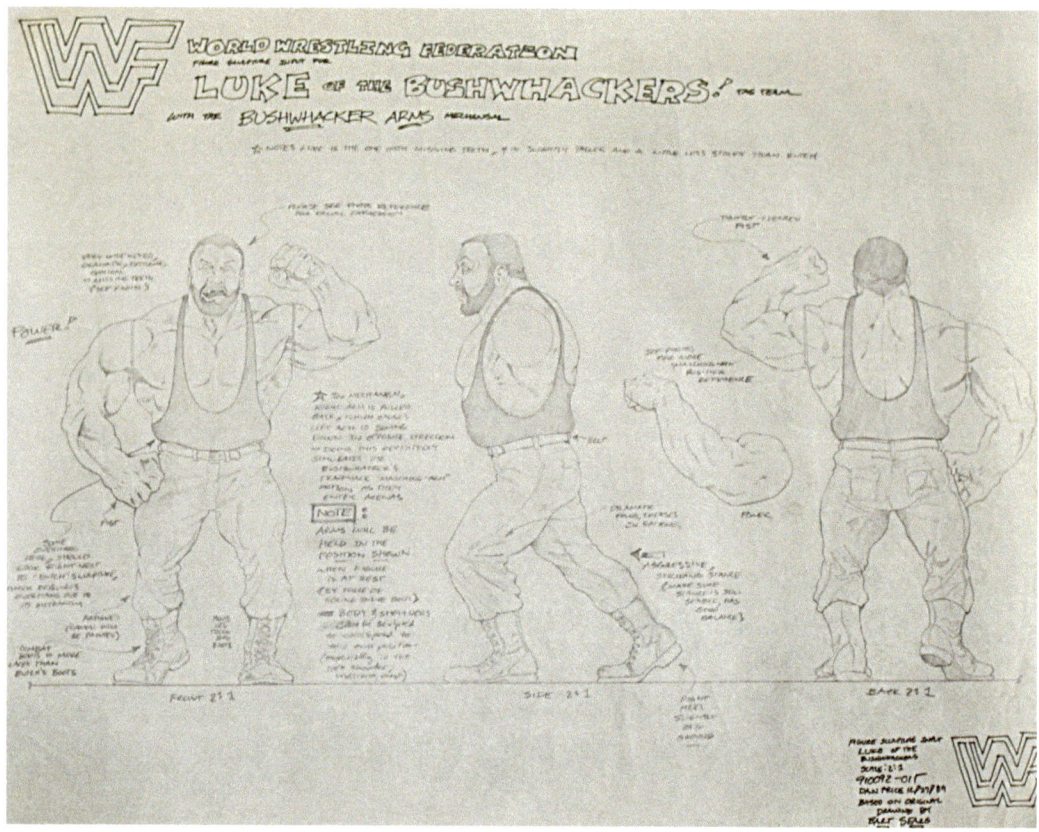

Drawings
Early parts of the production process had the art design team draw up designs deciding how and what mechanism the wrestling figure would have. Here the Bushwhackers sketch is designed by Bart Sears, which gives in-depth detail, from facial expressions to the mechanisms used.

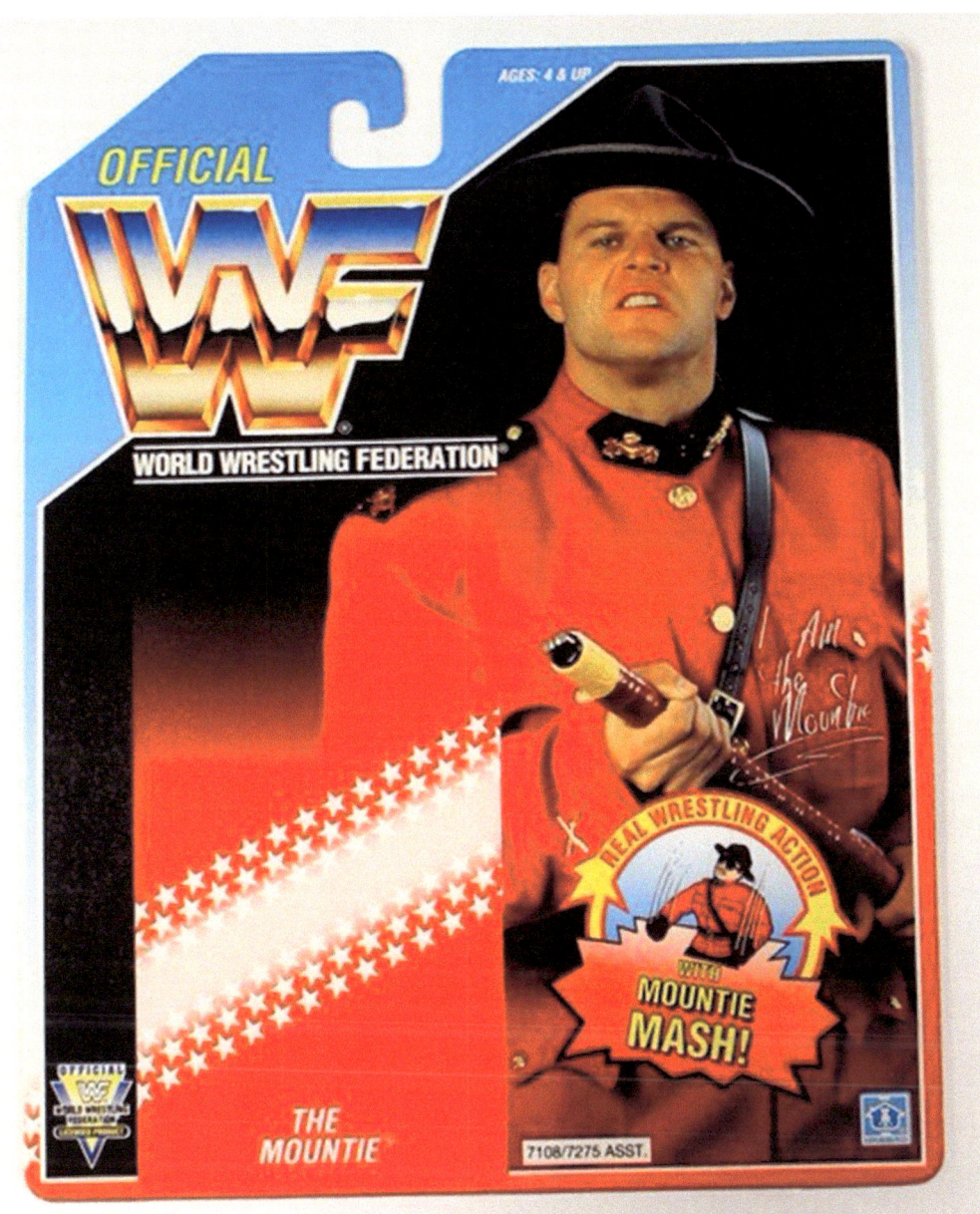

Backing Cards
Here is a backing card sample (proof card). Tests were carried out to see which designs were practical, and edits could easily be made. The packaging was often better than the action figure, which played such an important role. These images were kindly supplied by Rene Hajek.

Prototypes and Two-ups

Pictured above is a prototype of Bret 'The Hitman' from series 4. All forms of the prototype can be used and there is no set code. Various materials like resin, urethane or even repaints and the plastics from standard action figures were used. Pretty much anything to get that idea across. Two-up's replica of the Bret Hart prototype is twice the scale. That's a whopping nine inches high. Only one action figure in the two-up scale would ever be created. It's debated whether series 11 had any at all.

Over the years plenty of test shots have arisen. They are the same size as your prototypes but usually a solid colour and unpainted. They were used for testing mechanisms, likeness and safety.

Other techniques had been used from the Hasbro team. Matt Cardona has pointed out the use of a wooden block to mould the plastic bubble, then a colour-coding scheme booklet had to be abided by. It could take close to twelve months to produce one action figure. Most toys were created by hand in 1990, unlike today where a 3D printer and computer technology can speed up the process by at least six months. An awful lot of workmanship went into the manufacturing, which shows the great skills Hasbro had.

Series 6

Berzerker (with tunic)
Ric Flair
El Matador
Papa Shango (with bones)
Tatanka
Repo Man

Series 6 would be the last series with the traditional blue, white and red background on the backing card. Around this time series 6 had huge availability and decent amounts were sold worldwide. By now the foreign language backing cards had ceased and that left us only with the English language backing card.

Heavy repurposing of action figures is seen for the first time. Bezerker borrows its body mould from Hacksaw Jim Duggan, Tatanka is a remake of Texas Tornado, Ric Flair is a repurposed Ravishing Rick Rude toy, while El Matador is a reworked Jake 'The Snake' Roberts.

Although series 6 is made up of many regenerated parts, bits and moulds, we do see a fresh bunch of wrestlers added to the toy line. Bizarrely, as a youngster the repurposing was hardly noticeable.

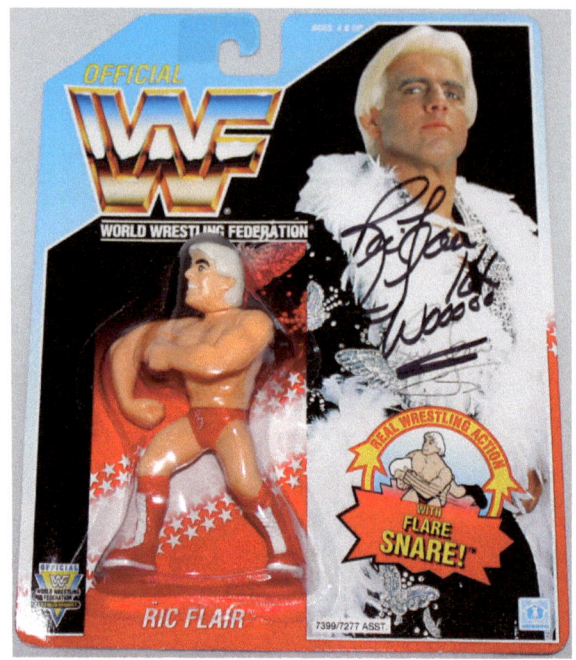

Ric Flair

Sixteen-time world champion Ric Flair needs no introduction to the world of wrestling. His lavish lifestyle comes to mind and his need for quality seeps through to this action figure. The ring trunks and boots match that from his later 1992/early 1993 run in. Ultimately, he lost a career-ending match with Mr Perfect. WWF Hasbro was not the only licensee manufacturing Ric Flair wrestling figures: World Championship Wrestling teamed up with Galoob to compete with the WWEs dominant market share. WCW Galoob toys could fill an entire book in itself but Ric Flair, among other wrestlers, orchestrated some lovely action figures.

Repo Man

This wrestling figure could easily fit into a batman play set as a villain. It's full of character and has that cheeky grin of a joker. That was the era we were in and wrestling was full of character in the early 1990s. Repo Man is another addition to the jumping action figures from the toy line, making him one of twelve of that type. He and the Warlord were the only two wrestling figures from the toy line to wear a mask.

Berzerker

The fabric tunic accessory covers over the reused body mould doing a great job in hiding the fact it was once used for Hacksaw Jim Duggan. The right hand is sculpted to fit the 2 x 4 accessory, but drawings do show plans for a sword and shield, showing the potential for it to be used in that way. The sword and shield were excluded from the final production – a missed opportunity. However, the brown tunic is demountable and is easily lost. Replacing the tunic can turn into a nightmare as not all survive.

Tatanka

One of the most popular toys from series 6. Enduring a near two-year undefeated run, Tatanka truly was a fan favourite. He wore some intricate ring attire and is proud of the native American roots. WWE Hasbro missed a trick here and should have gone full swing by including more. The tomahawk axe, feathered head gear and native apparel would have propelled the action figure further. Still making sporadic wrestling appearance globally, Tatanka will go down as a legendary wrestling character. Often, he would trek the globe just to entertain fans.

Papa Shango

Every child's worse nightmare, Papa Shango, the creepy voodoo master, often cast spells on his opponents, terrifying audiences. That element crept into the minds of children and owning the toy resembled that of witchcraft. The darker glances on the backing card is enough to put the creeps into anyone. The action figure must be up there with the best. The tattoos give it that extra bit of bite and the face work is spooky. Papa Shango used the bones to cast spells on opponents, so the role play included this too. Including a skull accessory, it could have done more harm than good as it may have frightened children.

El Matador

There's nothing drastic to add about the El Matador action figure in series 6. It's just a decent action figure that can be easily acquired. An evergreen and a loyal worker, fans appreciated Tito Santana's hard-working ethic. The smiling face brightens up series 6, plus the vibrant ring attire is accurately used. Executing the spring-loaded punch was always fun to operate.

Funskool

Although Hasbro are recognised as being the dominating wrestling figure producer, Funskool were a toy manufacturer for the Asian market. Funskool (India) Ltd contributed under license from the WWE and Hasbro.

With the agreement with Hasbro, Funskool used the same images and moulding techniques and produced wrestling action figures to a decent standard, copying the traditional ways. The materials used were never as solid, but the concept is still visible. The quality is noticeable as the backing cards were thinner and the plastics used made the action figures slightly flexible. It's safe to say Hasbro were the masters of toy manufacturing.

On a collector's point, finding WWE Funskool examples today is hard as not an awful lot have survived due to its poor quality.

With Funskool's lack in quality, it is difficult to maintain action figures in top condition. No official number has been noted or recorded regarding quantity made, leaving for a wide-open collectors' market, mostly yet to be discovered.

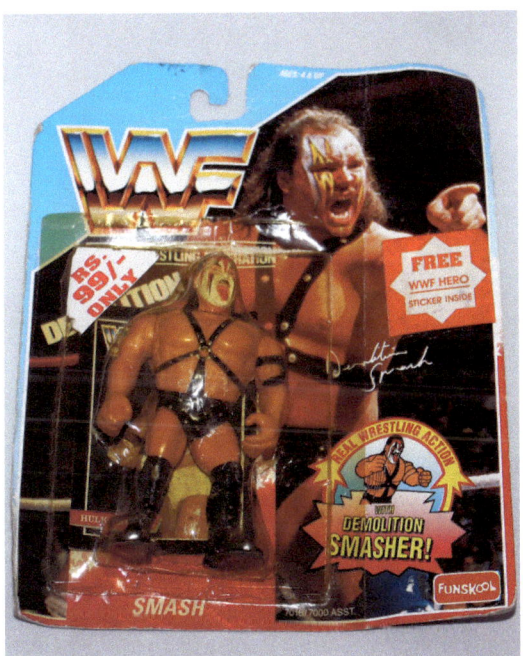

Smash
One of the easier Funskool action figures to find; notice the paper-like material used for the backing card. Also, the bubble is not a solid material compared to Hasbro's action figures. Every Funskool wrestling figure had a free sticker included.

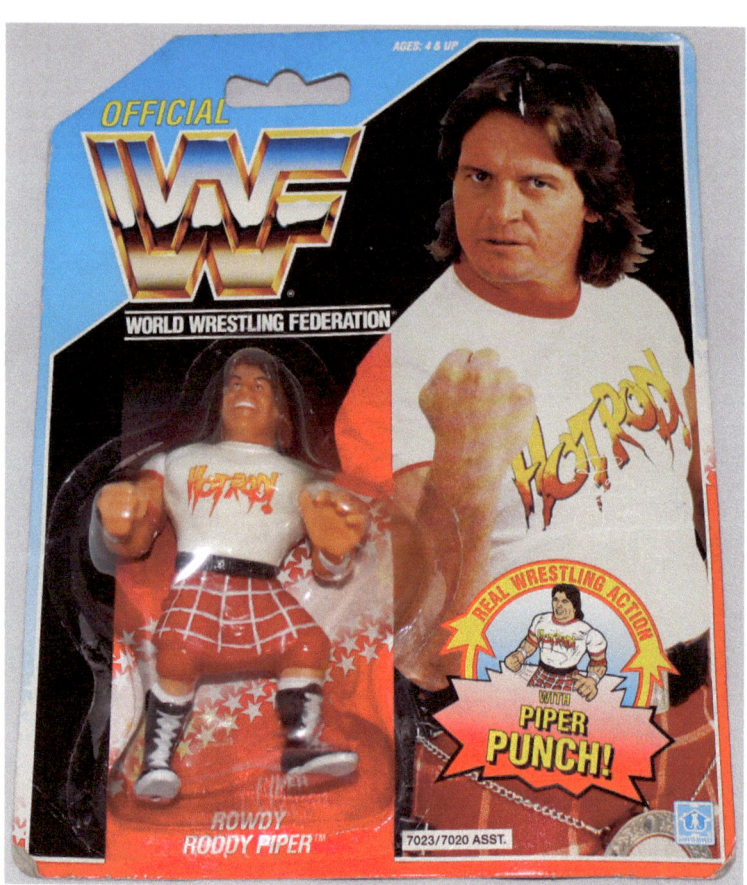

Rowdy Roddy Piper
You can see here that the action figure is lacking detail compared to the Hasbro action figure. The paint work difference is noticeable and the hair colour is lighter. The wrestling boots are all black without the white sole.

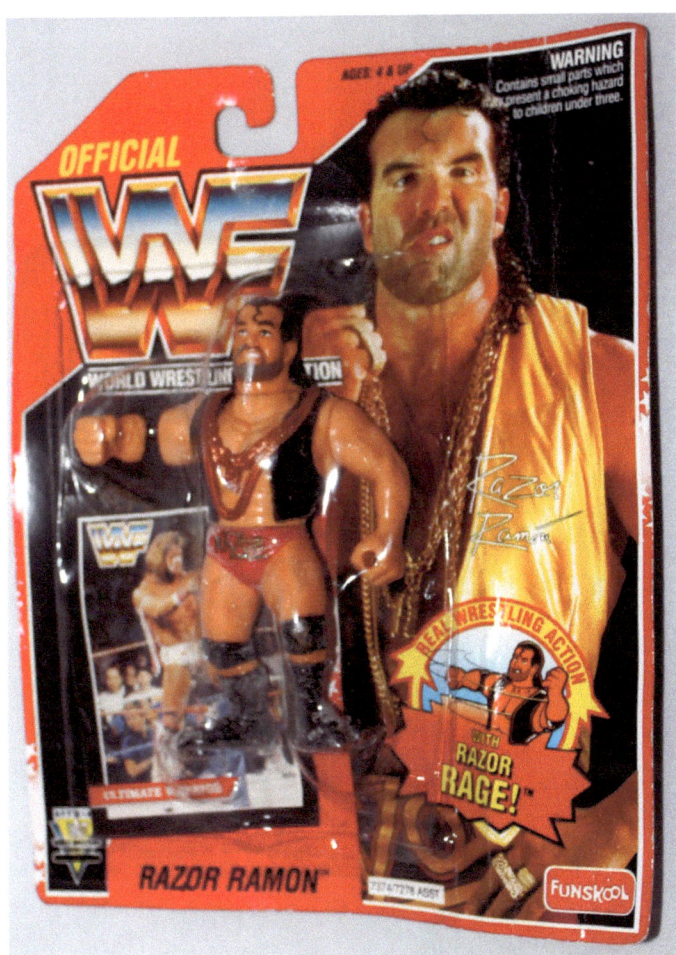

Razor Ramon
The same design as the series 7 Hasbro piece, a major difference is that instead of the usual yellow or dark-blue backing card, the Funskool version has a red backing card. There is a bronze chain included, which should be all gold.

Other action figures to surface from the Funskool line are listed below.
Million Dollar Man, Ted Dibiase (series 1)
Lex Luger
Ultimate Warrior (series 2).
Bam Bam Bigalow
The Undertaker (series 8)
Hulk Hogan (series 1)
Yokozuna (series 8)
Mr Perfect (series 3)
Macho Man Randy Savage (Series 5)

On each backing card and like the Hasbro line, they show which other wrestlers to collect. Images of Legion of Doom, Honky Tonk Man, the Nasty Boys, Hulk Hogan (series 2), Ted Dibiase (series 2), the entirety of series 1 and Shawn Michaels (Rockers) are visible. Unearthing of any more Funskool pieces is yet to happen.

Series 7

Kamala
Razor Ramon (with gold chains)
Shawn Michaels
Nailz
Owen Hart
Crush

The first series to change the colour of its backing card, each series prior to this had been produced with a red, white and blue theme. Aiming to attract more sales, the packaging changed to all yellow.

Series 7 gave us some exceptional wrestling talent and it appears it was ever so futuristic in its release in 1993. Shawn Michaels, Razor Ramon and Owen Hart shot to stardom in the mid- to late 1990s, Crush advanced notability as a respected bad guy in later years, while Kamala and Nailz make up the set.

Series 7 sees a recognised holy grail item in Kamala with a moon belly while collectors are still hunting down a lost prototype of Shawn Michaels. Either way, the series was a success and became the focus of massive sales.

Kamala

Let's start this chapter with one of the most talked about wrestling figures of the past twenty-five years, the holy grail of wrestling figures and the one which has the most rumours and questions: Kamala by Hasbro for the World Wrestling Federation. Pictured above is a standard release Kamala action figure from series 7. It's not particularly rare; in fact it's common and easily available. The focal point of this toy is the yellow star on the stomach of Kamala, something so small that changed the fate of toy collecting and has had wrestling fans talking for years. Expect to pay £50 ($70) for a mint on card standard release Kamala.

Plans were set for Kamala to have a yellow moon on his stomach instead of a star. It is thought that only twenty-four were made for factory use only, none made retail.

So why did WWF Hasbro halt procedures with the yellow moon versions? All sorts of reasons and rumours have circulated but nothing is definite. Rumours suggesting that the original design offended the Islamic faith or that WWE wanted it changed have all circulated. Nothing is sure, but if I was to guess it was possibly a factory error. If a factory worker had marked a large quantity with a yellow star instead of a moon by mistake, recalling that amount of stock becomes a job itself, let alone costly. Or it could have easily slipped through quality control. Until a member of the Hasbro or WWE comes forward and tells the story, the mystery will continue. No one has come forward and given an accurate enough reason for why it was changed.

In 2008, I had the privilege of meeting and talking to Kamala, who kindly signed my action figure, the popular version collectors love. A brief five-minute chat ensued, which ended in us both discussing the toy. I asked Kamala why the moon got left out on the action figure and his reply to me was, 'I really don't know, it just got left out'. From there Kamala specified that he in fact owned a moon-belly Kamala action figure, one of the twenty-four. Sadly, in the past ten years Kamala's health deteriorated, meaning the rare action figure he owned was sold to a collector to cover his medical bills.

If you're on the lookout for the 'holy grail' of wrestling figures, be prepared to pay around $25,000. Yes $25,000. Be wary of counterfeits. Telltale signs include tampered with blisters/backing cards, and check for glue residues, resealing and uneasy bumps around the plastic blister. Another thing, make sure no glue remains from a retail sticker mark – remember these items never made retail so there is no need for a pricing sticker. Finally, buy from a reputable collector/dealer; no cowboy auctions with blurry pictures and a shaky background story. If it's legit, the seller will have a lot of information so be sure to ask questions and make sure you feel comfortable with the transaction.

Razor Ramon

Within a short period of time Razor Ramon propelled himself from newcomer to main event player. His trademark gold and cocky style had every fan hating his guts. Turns out Razor Ramon was one of the best wrestlers of our generation. Hasbro carried on with that cocky swagger, with the smug-looking grin and gold chain accessory making for one of the toys of the 1990s. The finest detail is the hair straggle. There's no mistaking the action figure, and the Razor Rage clothesline manoeuvre is important too. If you are looking for a reason why these toys were the best of the decade then here's a fine example.

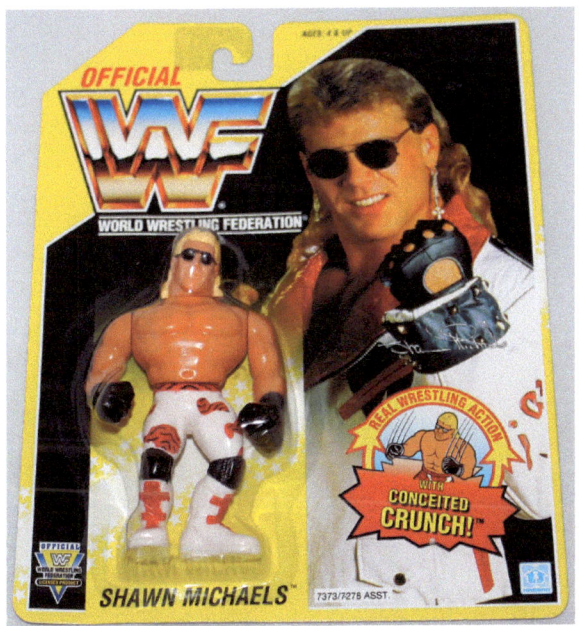

Shawn Michaels

To have the toys of the nineties, you need to include the wrestler of the nineties and we have that in Shawn Michaels, the Heartbreak Kid. Fresh from the breakup of The Rockers, Michaels conquered the singles division, winning over a worldwide fan base. Observant wrestling fans expected a totally different Shawn Michaels from the one received in series 7. Michaels is as conceited as ever but has a drawback punch similar to Jake 'The Snake' Roberts. The head sculpting and the ring attire has adjustments too. Instead, reused moulds from Macho Man No. 1 were used with a differently modelled head.

No sign of the magazine prototype Shawn Michaels has surfaced and there is not much information to match. There is still chance of the piece existing but the whereabouts is uncertain. Hopefully the work hasn't been destroyed. What does scare collectors is that if the piece surfaces at auction, it will surely generate huge interest.

Nailz
For all those who don't remember, Nailz played the character of an escaped convicted and feuded with the Big Bossman. Hasbro created an evil expression on Nailz faces and mastered the convicts wrestling attire. 902714, his prison number, is seen printed on the shirt. The wind-up punch mechanism known as the Jailhouse Jab shows who WWE and Hasbro were targeting these toys at, as today it's laughable to an extent. Also, they're missing a trick here by not including the nightstick.

Owen Hart
Owen Hart's figure was a great piece and it did truly lighten up the line. With a clothesline action, his blonde hair, zippy purple attire and checkered boots, it was a fine piece of one of wrestling's greats. The ring attire matches the era from when he competed as a singles athlete and in a tag team. Looking at Jim 'The Anvil' Neidhart from series 5, you will notice both attires look alike. Both made up the tag team, the New Foundation, and it is possible plans were drawn up at this time. A magazine shot pictures a prototype of Owen Hart with alternative leg sculpting. RIP Owen Hart.

Crush

The second Crush focuses on his rebranding as a good guy. It's a decent effort but it does have the expressions of a caricature toy. All is fair and it is a standard action figure in many ways, but maybe the moulding from Hulk Hogan series 2 would have been better. Having that mould could have replicated Crush and the finish move he executed in wrestling matches.

Series 8

Bret 'The Hitman' Hart
The Undertaker (with cloak)
Bam Bam Bigalow
Yokozuna
Lex Luger
Mr Perfect

Late 1993/early 94 and wrestling fans see the release of series 8, known generally as the red card series. The backing cards of the action figures changed to all red compared to the previous series 7 yellow card.

This is where we see the cost effectiveness coming into the production of the toy line. Three of the action figures (Bret Hart, Undertaker and Mr Perfect) were all given repainted ring attires for the release of series 8. Although repurposed, it doesn't stop series 8 from being an excellent line nonetheless.

The wrestling figure line peaked here, and everything thereafter was never fully the same. Simply the good vibes were missing afterwards.

Bret 'The Hitman' Hart

This series 8 action figure sees a repainted, upgraded ring attire for the legendary wrestler. Copying the Hart Attack wrestling action, this time around a more vibrant look shows off the hitman's look. What truly sets the series 8 action figure apart is the close detailing the figure received. A Hitman illustration logo has a deeper effect than the traditional heart emblem. However, the real winner is the skin tone. Series 4 Bret looked pale, and a darker skinned version brings the character to life.

A version seen by collectors as the holy grail of Bret 'Hitman' Hart wrestling figures has different coloured elbow pads and wrist bands. The basic series 8 figure has pink elbow pads and pink wrist pads. The most sought-after version has black elbow pads with white wristbands. It has been declared a prototype, which means it never made retail.

The Undertaker

In addition to the series 8 line, this Undertaker is equipped with a long dark-black cloak accessory, which could be removed, creating more mystery to the dead man's action figure. Bizarrely the hat mould was still firmly attached to the action figure as the work copies everything from the series 4 Undertaker. The paint tone is more appealing in series 8 too. Although the modelling is based on series 4, a collector can notice the difference between each Undertaker action figure. Series 4 has ginger hair while series 8 Undertaker has blacker hair. It is one of the most desired action figures in the entire line.

The red backing card makes the action figure stand out, a grim reaper glance portrait of the Undertaker as a living dead creature. That grey glove of his shadow's half of the slide photograph makes you want to step into the dead man's soul.

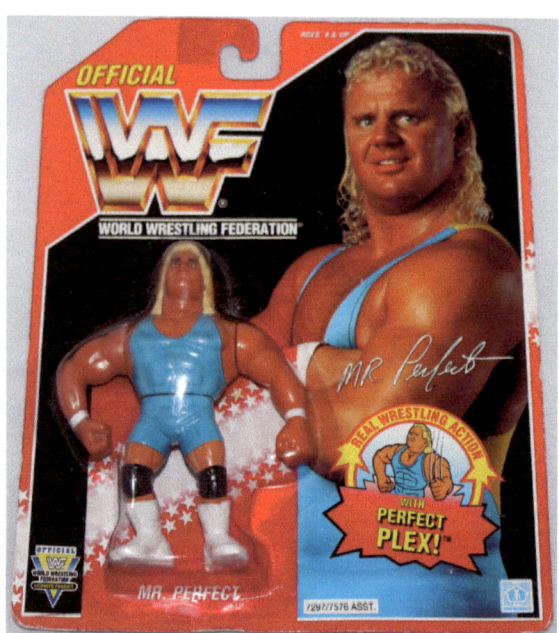

Mr Perfect

Still and forever, Curt Hennig will always be regarded as one of the best in-ring performers, with huge technical ability and a knack for talking. The action figure carries exactly the same figure moulding as the series 3 release. The series 8 Mr Perfect has different coloured ring apparel and is slightly harder to find loose. Known as the second action figure of Mr P., the attire is dark-aqua blue on the front, with distinguished yellow triangle on the back of the costume. We also see the white wrestling boots with 'Mr P' inked on each foot.

Yokozuna

Easily the largest of all action figures released from the line, in all it's an excellent representation of the sumo wrestler. It reached retail in mid- to late 1993, around the time he was world champion. The Sumo Splash manoeuvre is exquisite and shows the cartoon era wrestling was entering. Take a closer look at the expression on the face of the action figure; does that look like an angry expression? This shows how Yokozuna's figure was depicted as a villain.

    If I had to say which WWE Hasbro wrestling figure would achieve higher value in the collectors' market, it's this one. Why? Well collectors appreciate rare pieces and have invested heavily in the green series, pieces of which have already been discovered. Yokozuna from series 8 can still be located at a reasonable price still, though not an awful lot remain fully intact or even still MOC. Search carefully and the bargains are right in front of you.

Lex Luger
Yes, body parts are reused but that's not stopping this being an excellent addition to series 8. The head sculpting is sublime and then the ring attire is a spot-on match. If you look at the wrist bands, Union Jack engravings have been painted over. Why? The arms are taken from the original series 4 British Bulldog action figure. Also, the legs are taken from a series 3 Hulk Hogan action figures. All repainted, all making up the Lex Luger action figure. Whether you call it cheap or clever, it works well.

Bam Bam Bigalow
An accurate action figure showing the unusual look of Bam Bam Bigalow. The head tattoo stands out, even though his arms replicate the tattooed body. Then look at the flamed costume. Only a wrestling figure could come with such features. Its fine detail shows the character the creative studios of the global wrestling companies gave us. Adding the tattoos to this wrestling figure was not a hard task. A simple a stencil or spray would be used, and a push pad is likely to have been used on the arms. A quick dab on to the targeted area created a detailed finish.

Accessories and Other Goodies

Not only did wrestling fans get their hands on the 4.5-inch action figures, other wrestling accessories were also available at that time. Although the majority of the larger items were geared up for role play, there are some whacky and unusual items out there. Pictured below are some of the goodies on the market, though there is no picture of a three-wheeled trike, which became available through Playskool. Because wrestling in the 1990s was major business, there are possibly more pieces out there that have yet to be discovered.

Bop Bags
Three 48-inch inflatable bop bags of the Ultimate Warrior, Hulk Hogan and Jake Roberts were fun, especially as these were ideal for grappling against.

Championship Belt
Contributing more fury to the fight, the heavyweight championship title belt became a popular accessory to own. Casting yourself as the champion and imitating wrestling heroes gave you that extra bit of confidence in yourself. Expect to pay £100 for mint in box.

Trace Plates
Extraordinary trace plates introduced the 1990s youth to the art world. After all, wrestling is theatre at its best. Pointless some might say, but WWE and Hasbro were striking while the iron was hot. Included are six trace plates and a case box. Ultimate Warrior, Hulk Hogan, Legion of Doom, the Nasty Boys, Big Bossman, Sgt Slaughter, Ricky Steamboat, Rowdy Roddy Piper, The Rockers, Earthquake, Ted Dibiase and The Undertaker make up the set.

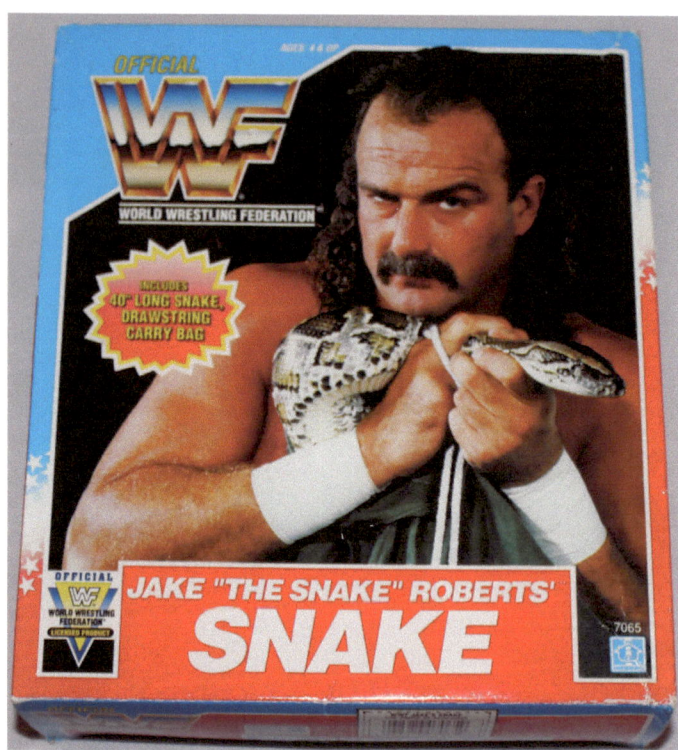

Damien
As Damien became a fan favourite pet snake, alongside Jake 'The Snake' Roberts, it was only right to produce a 40-inch-long replica. Here he enters the merchandise world as possibly the only ringside pet to ever do so. The best part of the Damien snake toy was recreating the role play of Jake 'The Snake' Roberts, and as a youngster it became a frightening experience. To add controversy to the Damien toy, he was lacking the thickness and he is grey and not green and black like a python. Was Damien reused from a different Hasbro line? Quite possibly.

Action Figure Carry Case
An action figure carry case had been available throughout the period, which does exactly what it says on the tin and is used for the standard 4.5-inch action figures. This accommodates twenty-four action figures officially. It's blue and measures 13 inches in height and 11.5 inches wide with a depth of 6 inches. It protected wrestling figures from getting bashed around. Although not essential, it served a purpose.

Hulk Hogan Wrestling Gear
Enclosed in the package is a Hulk Hogan T-shirt, headband and two wristbands, all so that you can portray your wrestling hero and to give children the chance to dress just like Hulk Hogan. It's an interesting novelty piece. Hulk Hogan foreign language wrestling gear exists, which is bigger and better than the English language release and exhibits a more accurate likeness to Hulk Hogan. GIG distributed the 'il Vero Costume de Hulk Hogan' to Italy in 1991. With limited units available and rarely found on online auction sites, I'm not willing to estimate a value.

Ultimate Warrior Wrestling Gear
Comparable to Hulk Hogan's wrestling gear, we see an Ultimate Warrior T-shirt, mask, two armbands and four tassels. Even though Hulk Hogan's wrestling gear was not much to write home about, the Ultimate Warrior version is even less appealing and was a poor effort.

Talking 12-inch Wrestlers

Only two 12-inch talking wrestling figures were made. Whether plans were made for more is uncertain. Would fans have wanted more? Surely an Undertaker or Bret 'Hitman' Hart 12-inch talking figure would have sold well. The pull-string chord on the back of each figure echoes famous quotes and catchphrases they once used. With age, the sound can muffle. It is best kept mint in box – that's if you can find one that is.

Series 9

Rick Steiner
Scott Steiner
Doink The Clown
'Hacksaw' Jim Duggan (with USA flag)
Tatanka
'Million Dollar Man' Ted Dibiase

The key difference for series 9 is the purple-coloured backing card. Hitting shops around early 1994, it copied series 8 in repurposing the toys, but that is not all. Hereafter, the line did suffer in terms of availability and finding series 9 became a chore compared to previous series. The series alters from its advertisements due to unforeseen changes and variations to the ring attire. Not only this but a third Brutus Beefcake toy was scrapped halfway through production.

'Hacksaw' Jim Duggan

A second release of 'Hacksaw' Jim Duggan begins series 9. This time the ring attire is completely different from the traditional trunks and boots worn in series 2. The 2 × 4 accessory was excluded but instead an American flag was its replacement. Over moulding had been used to create the blue tank top pictured here, plus there is more colour on offer here. Other than the mentioned changes, the same structure to the toy works in comparison to the series 2 Hacksaw Jim Duggan.

The American flag accessory holds high value today. Over years the accessory could be damaged or lost, so seeking a replacement can become a task in itself. Dare I say the flag accessory is worth more than the action figure.

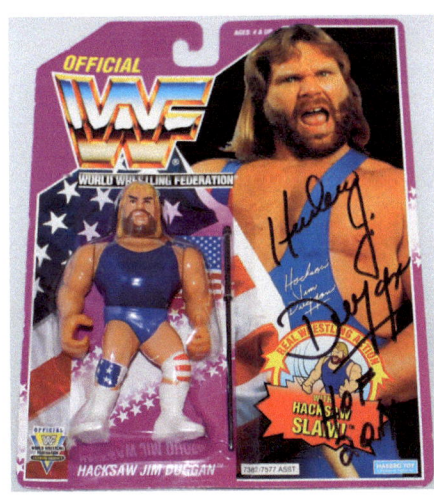

Scott Steiner

Albeit still together as a tag team, the decision was made to release tag teams as a separate entity from here on, rather than in the twin tag team sets fans became use to. Easy pickings for the designers here; the body mould had already been cast for Mr Perfect and Crush (series 7), so all it took was a new head sculpt and a quality repaint. The action figure works well for Scott Steiner and no complaints can be made.

Rick Steiner

Rick's attire appears vibrant and whacky, offering a patterned ring attire, and the earmuffs with a goatee is a well-designed feature. Adjustments to the boot colouring should be noted. Red and white boots were expected but the standard release has all red. Nobody wanted just one half of the Steiner Brothers, so it's logical to have both. Rick Steiner was the harder of the two to obtain and even today collectors are prepared to pay more than they would for his brother Scott.

Doink The Clown

Altering from the advertisement poster, Doink's leggings are all red and he's equipped with black boots. Fans were anticipating a completely different lower half. Advertisements show all-green tights and white knee pads with red stars, but reasons for the change are uncertain. The upper half makes up for the change as everything there is within proportion, and the green fuzzy hair is an exceptional effort.

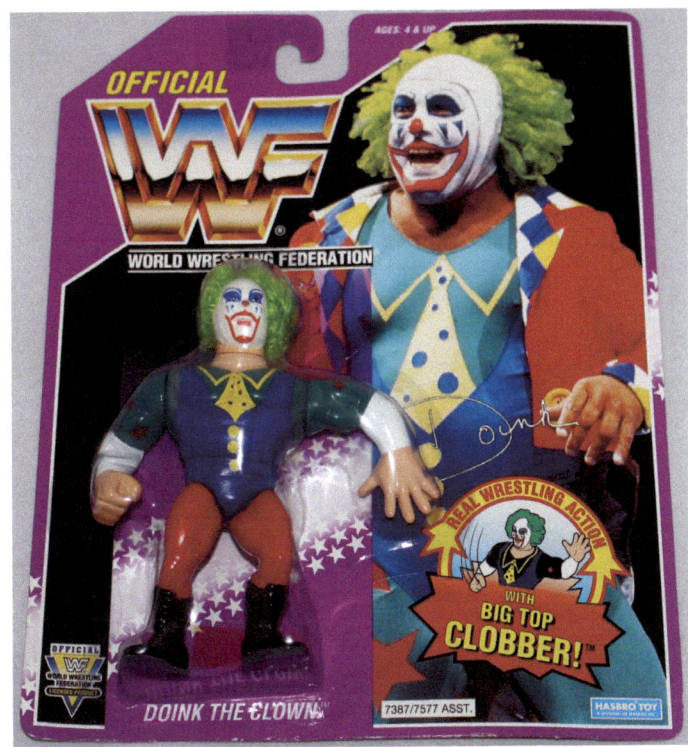

'Million Dollar Man' Ted Dibiase

The last of three WWE Hasbro wrestling figures produced on Ted Dibiase, and a quality addition in my opinion. No luxurious tuxedo, no Million-Dollar belt, just Ted Dibiase at his best, decked in his grappling gear and ready for action. To collectors in 2008, when comparing all Ted Dibiase action figures, the Series 9 Ted Dibiase is at the top of the value tables; in 2019 that has changed, as series 1 has equivalent value. That's why it's hard to value action figures – everything has ups and downs.

Tatanka

The same Tatanka action figure from series 6 was quickly bought back and rushed into the purple series 9 lot with no differences other than the backing card colour.

It is unknown why this decision was made. The variant coloured backing cards carries the same value.

Brutus 'The Barber' Beefcake

Toy fans were left disappointed when the scheduled third Brutus Beefcake action figure was halted halfway through production. Pictured wearing red and yellow leggings and in the same cast as the series 3, Brutus Beefcake's action figure was neither seen nor heard and fans were left wondering. Brutus Beefcake made a swift exit from the company in mid-1993, so plans were immediately stopped. Collectors pondered the whereabouts of the prototype image for years until 2015 when images appeared online. Suspicion was raised, but everything seems in order and to date there is two known prototype examples. Are there more? The mystery continues.

Series 10

Razor Ramon (Black attire with gold chain)
Razor Ramon (Purple attire with gold chain)
Shawn Michaels (White attire)
Shawn Michaels (Black attire)
Giant Gonzalez
Marty Jannetty No. 2
Bushwhacker Luke No. 2 (with hat)
Bushwhacker Butch No. 2 (with hat)
Samu
Fatu

Series 10, otherwise known as the blue card series, happened to be the penultimate series for the great toy line. Also, it would be the last line where the action figures were easily obtainable. The backing card changed to a darkened blue and in total, ten of our wrestling greats were there to choose from. The batch would reach the UK in mid-to late-1994. By that point, wrestling had changed from a widely loved sport to a lacklustre one. The fan base changed, and many people were losing interest in these wrestling figures as well. Hasbro was going through all sorts of changes to try to compete in the toy industry. The year 1994 would see it drop WWE and GI Joe, two of its huge brands. Everything was changing just before the dawn of the internet.

Shawn Michaels

Two versions to Shawn Michaels were produced for series 10, as pictured. Above is a newer black tights version and below is a re-released red and white tights version. Both action figures have the same mechanism move and the backing cards are identical. However, the rear of the backing card advertises the series 7 set instead of the series 10. The black tights version is considerably rarer loose, while both hold the same respect mint on card. Adding to this, the black tights version was extremely hard to find as it was non-existent in the UK, which was bizarre as both Shawn Michaels and Razor Ramon were top-draw wrestling talent.

Razor Ramon

Copying Shawn Michaels, Razor Ramon suffered the same fate and had two versions released for series 10. A rarer purple attire toy is pictured on top and the re-release from series 7 is pictured just below. Both toys were identical, except they had different ring attires. Even the gold chain accessory was included with both. Following suit, the purple attire Razor Ramon is worth more loose compared to the series 7 re-release, but both hold the same value mint on card.

Again, the rear of the backing card copies that of series 7. I'll also add that several Razor Ramon action figures made retail with many errors, from mis-painted arm pads to half-shaded beards. Rumours have surfaced suggesting that the rarer Shawn Michaels and Razor Ramon action figures were set for mail away special promotions. Small snippets in magazines have been noted, but there is no solid background to back this up. However, my question lies with why there were two versions? Was it an error? Was it cost effective? Were the toys rushed? Until answered by management, fans will not know for certain.

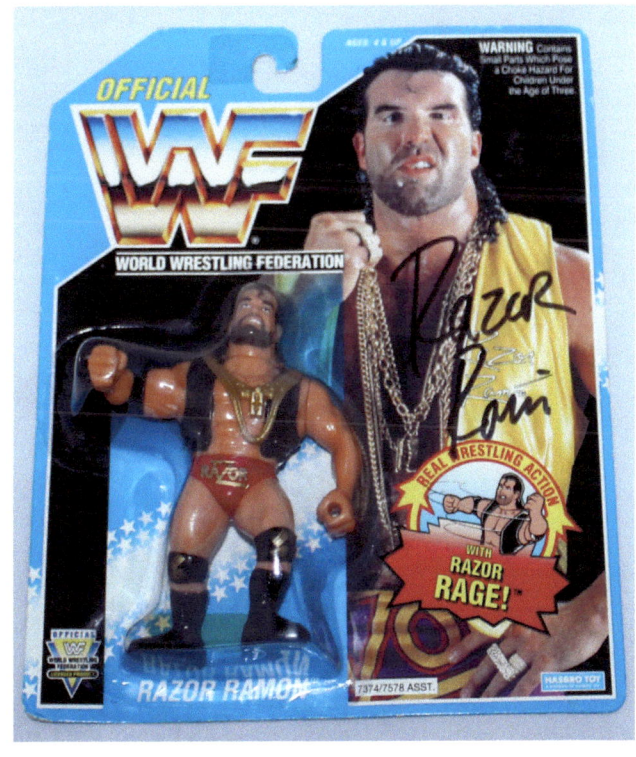

Giant Gonzalez
By far the most original and best from series 10, the body moulded fur and the giant's angry expression makes the toy appear to stand head and shoulders above the rest. Funnily enough, the action figure is roughly 1 cm taller than all others, making this truly a gigantic masterpiece and possibly one of the most accurate action figures ever made. Pushing the feet down sets off Gonzalez's wrestling rage. He was frightening enough, and this likeness is what made the toy so enjoyable.

Marty Jannetty
By this time, the line was going through a lull and nothing original reached fans in series 10. The body moulds were used on several wrestlers and the line was crying out for fresh ideas. Adding to that, the head mould is not the best, plus the teeth were left unpainted. In all, this toy was a let-down. The ring attire was well done, but everything else, even as a child, didn't feel right. This one definitely deserved better, especially as Marty Jannetty was a crowd pleaser.

The Bushwhackers: Butch (left) and Luke (right)
The second batch of the Bushwhackers sports an upbeat ring apparel and removable hats. This time the actions figures were sold separately instead of in a tag team twin pack. A clever move here was simply to switch heads to different body moulds. So, the Luke head sculpt was moved over to Butch's body mould and vice versa. This simple trick fooled many collectors, but both had the same build and they were often mistaken in their wrestling matches. Capitalising on this made for easy work for the design team. Sought after, compared to their previous design, and desired due to the hat accessories, be cautious of custom-made hat accessories – collectors want the genuine article.

Headshrinkers: Samu (left) and Fatu (right)
It's hard to tell the difference between the Headshrinkers; it's only the name printed on each action figure's leg that identifies each. They used repurposed parts to create the tag team and both are accurately tanned. Both have jumping action moves and lack creativity. Setting at least one of them apart would have helped. Both are readily available and easily purchased. Possibly the lowest values carded action figures, check for cracks and bubbles as that happens frequently here.

Series 11

The 123 Kid
Evil Crush
Yokozuna
Ludvig Borga
Bart Gunn
Billy Gunn
Adam Bomb

Series 11, typically named the green card series, is the final chapter of this great toy line. Manufactured in 1994, it would be early 1995 that saw it reach retail. All action figures from series 11 have a hefty price tag and that goes for mint on card or loose.

There's no real reason to explain why they are rare other than the fact that low numbers were produced. Certainly, in the UK the green-carded series was low to non-existent, while in the States pockets of areas had their fair share. Other countries suffered the same fate as the UK and to some collectors the green series was not heard of until the birth of the internet.

As the line was winding up, it seemed as if the plug had been pulled on the deal and they just went through the motions of producing series 11. An awful lot of repurposing is seen and on top of that, two action figures (Yokozuna and Crush) are mere repaints. Whether the line was halted abruptly is unknown, but it sure felt that way.

It is likely that at this time two-ups, which were previously made for every action figure, were stopped and Hasbro decided to just mould the head sculpt and ignore the entire body. That was due to financial cutbacks. Funnily enough, no two-up action figures have surfaced from series 11 or even series 10, so the likelihood is that the claim is legitimate.

It is likely sales were down and the dwindling interest in the line left only one option. Time plays its part too, as fans were growing older and the WWE Hasbro line stopped being toys and turned into collectors' items. That's why more are seen mint on card than loose. Forever thankful, all things must come to an end.

Yokozuna

Everything about series 11 Yokozuna replicates that of the series 8 release except for a change to the ring attire. A white ring attire replaces the previous red.

123 Kid

Possibly the rarest and hardest to find of all standard release wrestling figures from this toy line. You could go as far as to say that it is one of the rarest action figures ever produced. The flashy costume layout and the caricature facial mould are a sure winner here. Also, the green backing cards look better. For all the old school wrestling fans out there, you may recall the shock victory the 123 Kid achieved over Razor Ramon. The unheard-of youngster leaped from the top rope with a somersault and hustled a three count on the 17 May 1993 episode of Monday Night Raw.

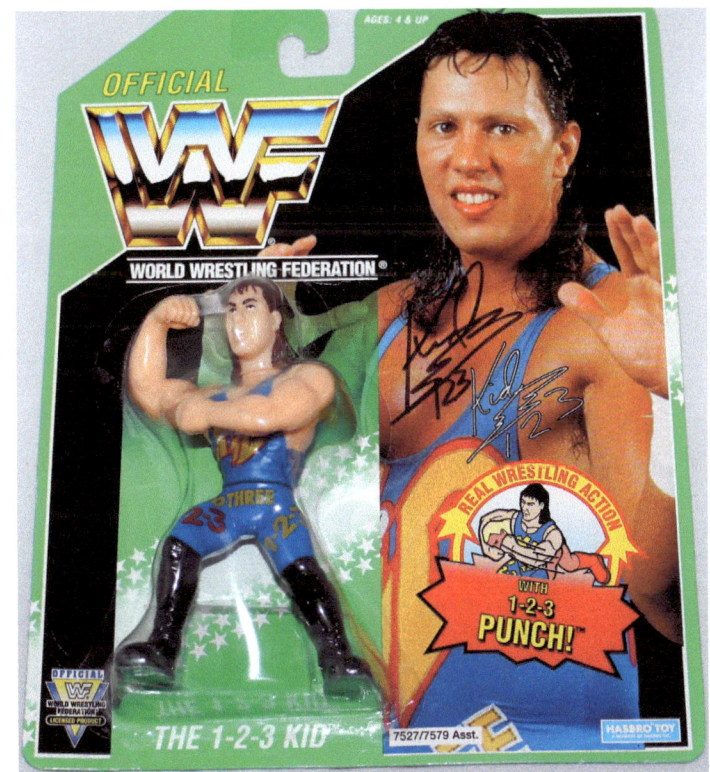

Bart Gunn

The Smoking Gunns are the final tag team from this great toy line and each was sold individually. Both hold the same value and respect in terms of rarity. The first thing you will notice with Bart Gunn is that the entire body of the action figure is taken from the Razor Ramon toy. The manufacturers may as well have gone one step further and included the gold chains. Other than that, it's a fair effort.

Billy Gunn

It's hard to tell each apart, as it's only the hair colour that is different. You can see from here that the line had that stale look about it; fresh mouldings and new movements were needed if the line was to progress. Like his brother Bart, it's a decent effort but does it offer that much? Sadly no.

Ludvig Borga
An accurate account of Ludvig Borga, the ring costume is the winner here. Although simple, it works well. The Finnish flag was imprinted all over and shows exactly who it is and what he's about. Having the Finland Finisher manoeuvre, which replicates a body slam, complements the toy. The mohawk haircut and the despondent facial expression were a bonus.

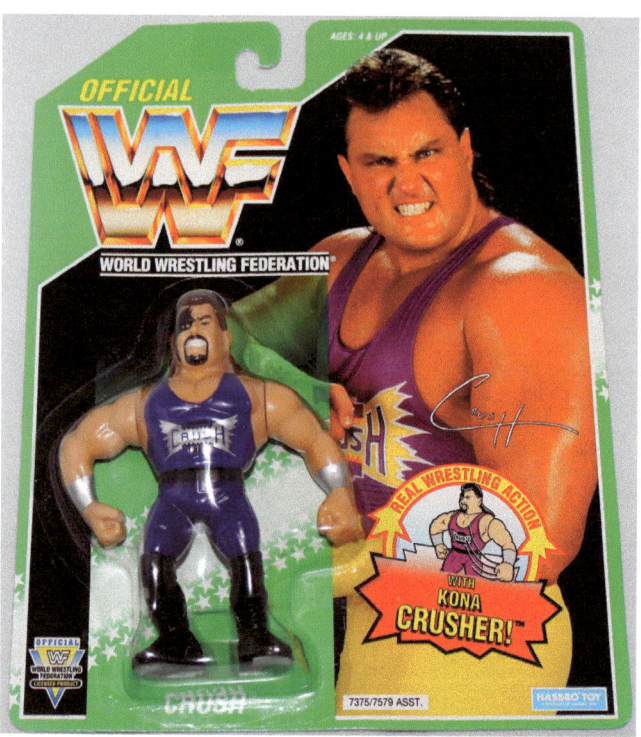

Evil Crush

Carrying on with the same modelling of the series 7 Crush, we see a totally different paint job, including the face paint. The same manoeuvre mechanism applies, but this time we see a green backing card. The action figure is interesting. The photograph slides of Crush used are from his times as a fan favourite, while the action figure has him wearing wrestling gear from his new bad-guy approach. The biography information interprets Crush as a good guy too, so there is a bit of a mash-up going on with the production here.

Collectors refer to this Crush series 11 toy as 'Evil Crush'. There's no visible reference to class it as Evil Crush; in fact 'Evil' is missing completely, so where that name came from is uncertain. Fans possibly use the 'Evil' reference to identify between the two.

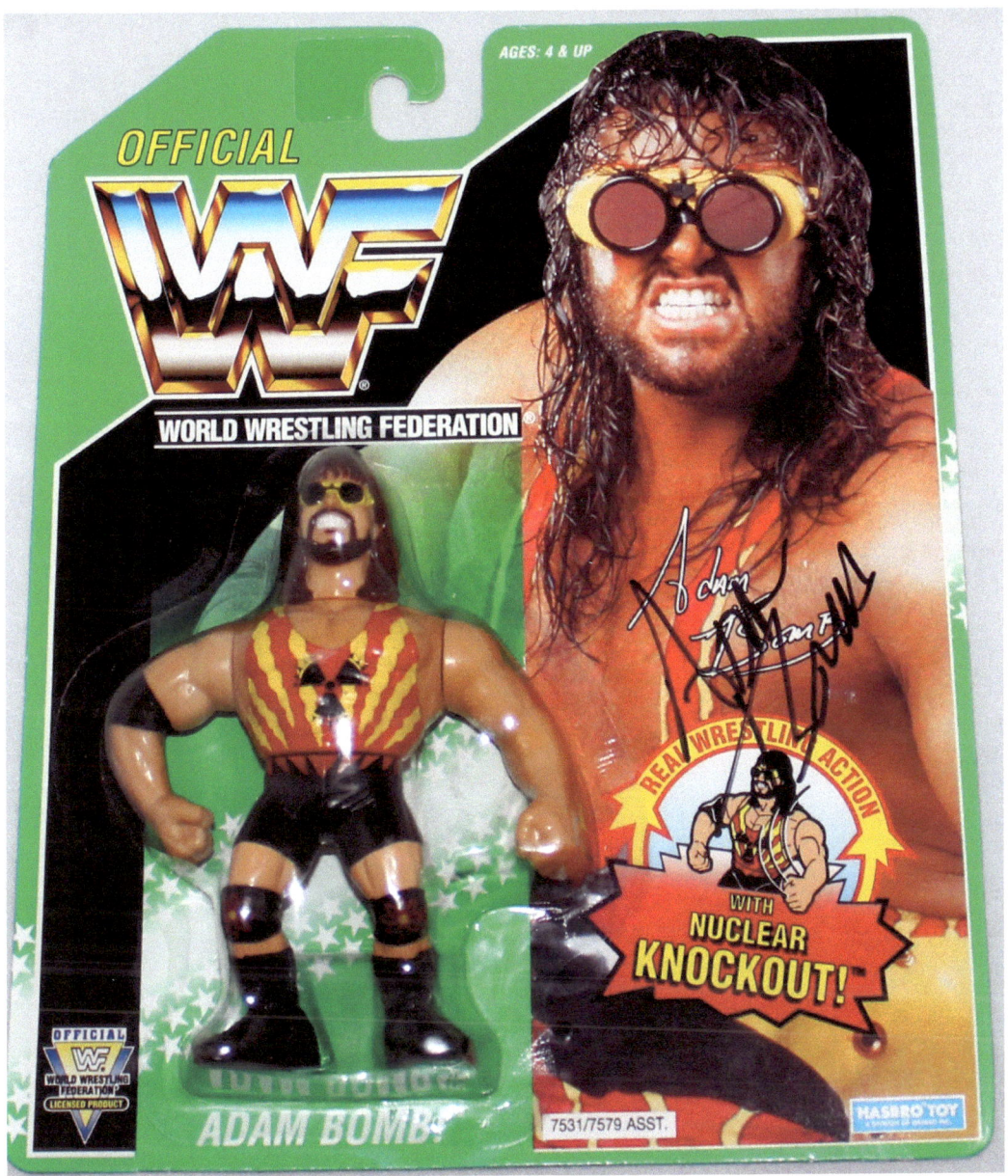

Adam Bomb
One of the last figures produced, it is one of the finest when it comes to likeness with truly great colours. Finely detailed ring attire shows the perfectionism Hasbro produced. Give credit to the Hasbro employees who would design, draw, sculpt or even paint them. Think of the quality they produced on an almost daily basis, whether it be for the WWF, Barbie, GI Joe or whomever. It has been said the skilled Hasbro artists could go about their job with ease and produce incredible detail at the click of their fingers. Here is a fine example of this. To top this off, the Real Wrestling Action really hits home with a cartoon, gimmick-like effect with a Nuclear Knockout! Safe to say, these toys were directly aimed at children.

Mail Away/Bagged Action Figures

Several exclusive mail away/bagged action figures surfaced during the period and now spawn huge interest from collectors as low numbers of each action figure were available. The most popular and loved mail away action figures came about due to an advertisement in the late 1994 issues of the World Wrestling Federation magazines. Hulk Hogan, Bret 'The Hitman' Hart and The Undertaker are the only three offered in the promotion.

Each action figure cost $7.95 plus postage in 1994, the main audience being the USA, which meant only a very small number reached other parts of the globe. Today an Undertaker or Bret 'The Hitman' Hart mail away action figures is likely to set you back close to $1,500 apiece. Not bad for a $7.95 investment.

Hulk Hogan Mail Away Exclusive
Here we show a loose version of the mail away example. More desired and harder to obtain is a sealed-in-bag Hulk Hogan magazine exclusive, which is numbered 81131 on the front. The action figure copies the design of the popular series 3 effort. However, with a different attire, this mail away exclusive shows Hulk Hogan wearing his ring attire from his return in 1993.

It is rumoured that slightly higher numbers were produced compared to the other two action figures offered in the promotion. Only in recent years has the value increased sharply from a mere £75–100 (sealed in bag) in 2008 to now hitting close to £500–600 ten years later in 2018.

Undertaker Mail Away Exclusive
One of the rarest wrestling action figures on the market fetches between £1,500–2,000 in 2019. The hard part is identifying a mail away from the standard series 4 and series 8 Undertaker action figures. The mail away version has a lighter brown beard and hair colour compared to a dark brown beard and hair colour for series 8 and the ginger/red beard and hair colour for series 4. The slight variation to the facial and hair colour attracts the collectors.

A mail away Undertaker is best kept in its original bag, stored away and well looked after. The original bag has the pin number 81133. Many collectors will not accept a loose mail away action figure and only opt for it being sealed in its original bag.

Bret Hart Mail Away Exclusive
Firstly, with this Bret Hart mail away exclusive, the advertised action figure offered a pink vest with black tights and alternative wrist and elbow pads. The version photographed above is the one received. Secondly and more important is the purple heart fiasco that surrounds the figure. It is uncertain whether a number had been released mint on card as well as bagged. Collectors welcome the bagged mail away as genuine, but most question whether the purple heart version being released mint on card is a mail away exclusive.

   For a safe bet with this mail away action figure, be sure to check for the pin number 81183. Look out for a slightly lighter skin tone, a purple heart, receding hairline and most of all make sure the action figure is still sealed in the original bag. The Undertaker mail away is barely noticeable without its bag and collectors will notice. An opened Bret Hart mail away does not pass as genuine with graders and collectors 99 per cent of the time.

Macho Man Randy Savage and Hulk Hogan Promotional Release
This promotion was one of the earliest known and they became available with the J. C. Penney wrestling ring exclusive offer. American retailer J. C. Penney offered the two action figures sealed in a bag separately and were included with the ring. They are a hugely desired part of the collection and fetch $2,000 today.

Hulk Hogan 2, UK Exclusive
Released via Silver Vision wrestling video distributions in the UK, the bag (pictured above) is usually packed with slightly more air and is slightly bigger. It has more written words compared to other mail away exclusives.

Macho Man Randy Savage Series 1 UK Exclusive
This figure is said to be available from a UK cereal promotion, possibly Shreddies or Shredded Wheat. Similar to the J. C. Penney Macho Man Randy Savage, it was available in a sealed bag. A 1989 Hasbro Gwent sticker should be easily visible. It is extremely hard to find and must be purchased from a trusted source as many fakes flood the market.

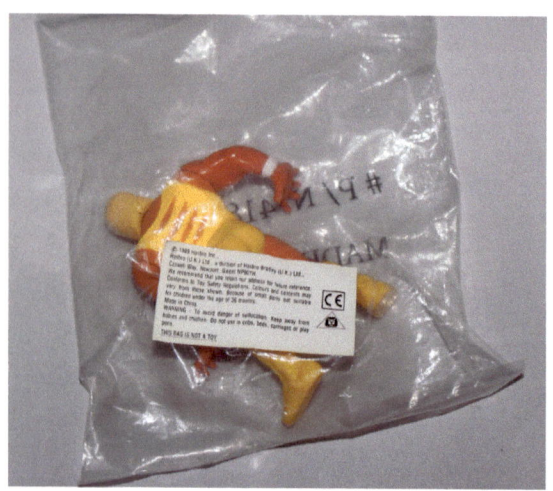 

Hulk Hogan 1 UK Exclusive
This figure was available again through the Shreddies or Shredded Wheat promotion just like Macho Man Randy Savage. More availability than Macho Man, they can be found online from time to time. Hulk Hogan being the main star of wrestling meant more action figures were produced. Many of the series 1 Hulk Hogan action figures got pushed for promotion and they became popular among wrestling fans. Check the bag for the correct labelling and be careful of scams and fakes. A 1989 Hasbro Gwent sticker should also be visible.

Other Mail Away Action Figures
It is likely that other mail away action figures were available at this time. Ultimate Warrior from series 1 was one of them. Talks of a Summer Slam 1992 promotion have surfaced too and I'm sure there were more than just that.

Dealing with mail away action figures is a tricky subject because it takes a lot of trust and there are unfortunately too many fakes available. If you are considering purchasing a mail away exclusive, then do be cautious of potential scam deals. Scammers will stop at nothing to take your hard-earned money. Ask a friend, talk to collectors, get opinions and above all use trusted payment methods and websites.

Series 12 and Beyond

Every WWE Hasbro fan and toy collector wants to know why the line came to an abrupt halt. Speculation exists and rumours abound but the stone-cold truth is that only WWE and Hasbro management know the real reason why.

With evidence recently arising regarding the series that never happened, we have a better idea now of what we might have seen. Images, sketches, head sculpts and word of mouth is the closest the fans will ever get to series 12.

Rumours have surfaced regarding which wrestlers were scheduled for release in series 12. Some of the names include Bastion Booger, Jeff Jarrett, Lex Luger, Doink The Clown, Diesel, Men on a Mission and even Bob Backlund has been mentioned.

The truth is, we will never know for certain. Past employees of the companies shed little light on the matter and sadly the line was discontinued. At the time, WWE was struggling to progress and it took several years to build up to the attitude era, and Hasbro also had its ups and downs. We do know Hasbro dropped its popular GI Joe real American hero toy line in 1994, so maybe a shake-up was occurring for both parties.

Since the discontinuation, a great following of wrestling fans and toy collectors globally remember and share stories about the wrestling figures. The inspirational collections fans own and share with us is hugely appreciated; long may that continue.

WWE Mattel Retro

Fast forward twenty-two years to 2016, and the world was surprised that WWE had teamed up with Mattel to produce a WWE Retro line. Everything to do with the WWE Mattel Retro line replicates the older toys pictured in this book. As of 2019, ten series featuring new and old wrestling legends have been produced. To say which era is the best is ridiculous, as both lots of wrestling figures do an exceptional job and each inspire their own special memories.

Pictured here is the brand-new WWE Mattel Retro Ric Flair action figure. Ending here is the official Retro ring. I've enjoyed collecting wrestling figures again after an extended break.

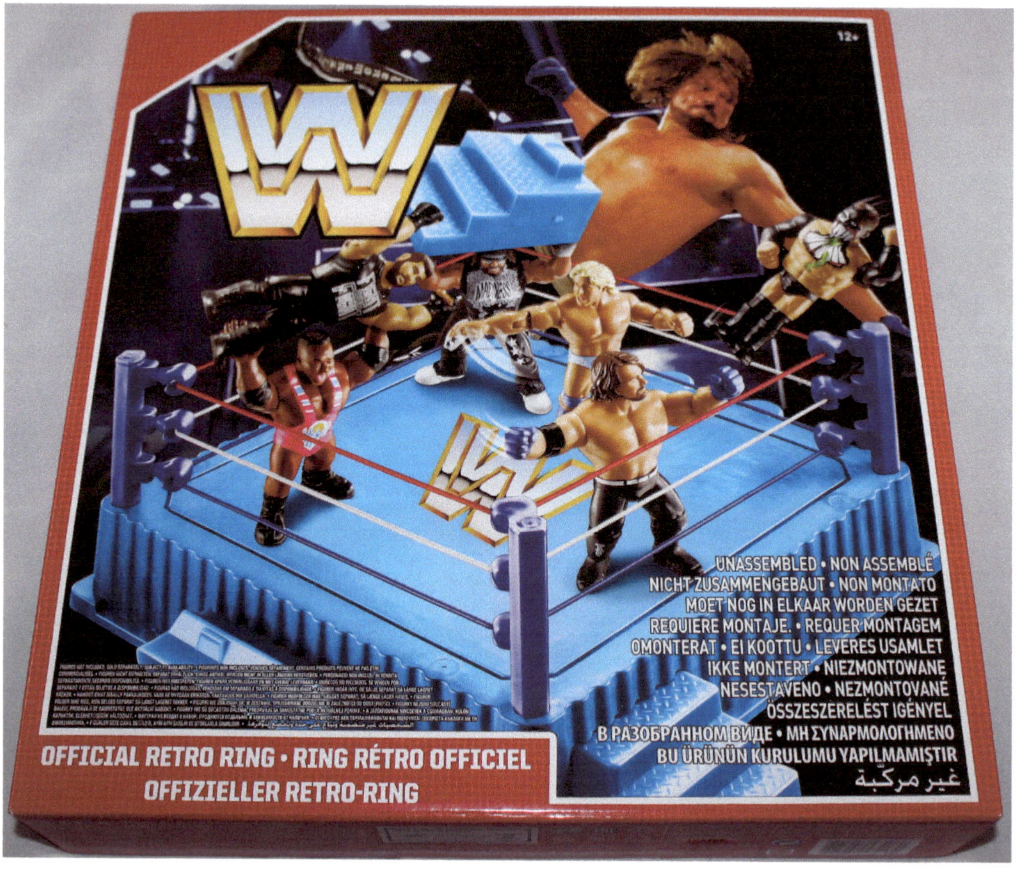